Overflowing with practical examples and guidance, *Lead Through Anything* is exactly what today's leaders need to navigate the uncertainties of the future with purpose, vitality, and agility. It's a timely and essential guide to becoming your best self as a leader.

### —JAY CONGER
Henry Kravis Chaired Professor of Leadership
Studies, Claremont McKenna College

Seale and Manfre have done incredible research on high-performing leaders and what they have in common. *Lead Through Anything* is the culmination of their work to impact the world of business, inspire leaders, and shape thriving organizational cultures.

### —TONY WOOD
Former CEO, Meggit PLC

*Lead Through Anything* outlines valuable principles for existing leaders and provides incredible guidance for those aspiring to leadership. Extensive research backs every strategic recommendation. All leaders will find valuable lessons that can immediately be put into practice.

### —RALPH G. KUECHLE, PHD
Clinical Psychologist and CEO, LooperRoom Inc.

Compelling, provocative, and accessible. The real stories of thriving leaders are inspiring, and the model makes their attributes feel teachable and attainable. The authors' masterful, meaningful use of language is elegant and energizing. I love this book!

### —ROSE GAILEY
Global Lead and Partner, Organization Acceleration
& Culture Shaping, Heidrick Consulting

*Lead Through Anything* uniquely distills the wisdom and experience acquired by countless leaders across sector, maturity, and geography. My own leadership journey has been elevated as a result of Dustin and Ed's work—many others will feel the same way.

### —ARJUN MALLIK
CEO, Prudential India Health

# LEAD THROUGH ANYTHING

### HARNESS PURPOSE, VITALITY, AND AGILITY TO THRIVE IN THE FACE OF UNRELENTING CHANGE

## DUSTIN SEALE & ED MANFRE

New York  Chicago  San Francisco  Athens  London  Madrid
Mexico City  Milan  New Delhi  Singapore  Sydney  Toronto

1 2 3 4 5 6 7 8 9   LCR   28 27 26 25 24 23

ISBN        978-1-265-50639-1
MHID        1-265-50639-6

e-ISBN      1-265-50667-4
e-MHID      1-265-50667-1

**Library of Congress Cataloging-in-Publication Data**

Names: Seale, Dustin, author. | Manfre, Ed, author.
Title: Lead through anything: harness purpose, vitality, and agility to thrive in the face of unrelenting change / by Dustin Seale and Ed Manfre.
Description: 1 Edition. | New York : McGraw Hill, [2024]
Identifiers: LCCN 2023024706 (print) | LCCN 2023024707 (ebook) | ISBN 9781265506391 (hardback) | ISBN 9781265506674 (ebook)
Subjects: LCSH: Leadership. | Diversity in the workplace—Management. | Employee motivation. | Trust. | Teams in the workplace.
Classification: LCC HD57.7 .S42863 2024 (print) | LCC HD57.7 (ebook) | DDC 658.4/092—dc23/eng/20230803
LC record available at https://lccn.loc.gov/2023024706
LC ebook record available at https://lccn.loc.gov/2023024707

McGraw Hill books are available at special quantity discounts to use as premiums and sales promotions or for use in corporate training programs. To contact a representative, please visit the Contact Us pages at www.mhprofessional.com.

McGraw Hill is committed to making our products accessible to all learners. To learn more about the available support and accommodations we offer, please contact us at accessibility@mheducation.com. We also participate in the Access Text Network (www.accesstext.org), and ATN members may submit requests through ATN.

# CONTENTS

## PART 3

# BRINGING THRIVING TO LIFE
# TODAY AND TOMORROW

# FOREWORD
## By Dr. Marshall Goldsmith

As lockdown began in March 2020 and the world grappled with the unprecedented challenges brought on by Covid-19, I found myself in a unique position. While many industries were reeling from the impacts of the pandemic, my work as an advisor and coach was in higher demand than ever before. CEOs, leaders, and organizations from all corners of the globe reached out, seeking guidance on navigating the storm and steering their companies away from disaster.

During this tumultuous time, Ed Manfre and Dustin Seale were sharing a similar realization. They observed a glaring gap in leadership training when it came to weathering major storms. While many leaders possessed the skills to handle day-to-day fires, they were ill-prepared to tackle the monumental crises that threaten companies and shake economies. Dustin and Ed recognized the pressing need for a comprehensive model that could equip leaders with the tools to address challenges both big and small.

In their book, *Lead Through Anything*, Ed and Dustin have taken on the formidable task of filling this void. Drawing from their extensive experience advising executives worldwide, they provide a refreshing perspective on leadership. They steer away from overwhelming checklists and instead offer a comprehensive model that simplifies the complexities of leadership and culture.

Through self-reflection and self-assessment, readers are encouraged to identify their strengths and areas for growth, empowering them to achieve equilibrium and become thriving leaders.

*Lead Through Anything* takes readers on a transformative journey, exploring each foundational principle of the Thriving state and providing practical methods for fostering a Thriving organizational environment. It delves into the three foundational principles of purpose, vitality, and agility. These principles are not only applicable during times of crisis, but are essential for fostering Thriving organizations in any circumstances. By embracing these principles, leaders can develop the resilience, adaptability, and foresight necessary to guide their teams and organizations through turbulent waters.

What sets *Lead Through Anything* apart in the realm of leadership development is Dustin and Ed's remarkable depth of experience in the field. Their genuine understanding of the challenges faced by leaders stems from their hands-on work with clients, assisting them in transforming their organizations from the inside out. This book transcends mere theories and case studies, as it is rooted in the real-world application of their model, witnessed time and time again. Their insights are not hypothetical, but rather grounded in the realities of leadership in action.

In a time where leadership is tested like never before, this book equips leaders with the tools, insights, and strategies needed to navigate complexity, inspire teams, and drive organizational success. I encourage every leader, whether seasoned or aspiring, to embrace the wisdom within these pages and embark on a transformative journey toward more effective and resilient leadership.

**Dr. Marshall Goldsmith** is the *Thinkers50* #1 Executive Coach
and *New York Times* bestselling author of *The Earned Life*,
*Triggers*, and *What Got You Here Won't Get You There*.

## PART 1

# THE CASE FOR THRIVING LEADERSHIP IN A DISRUPTED WORLD

# A Better Way

Roger Enrico and Martin Glenn sat in silence.

Roger, then head of PepsiCo Worldwide, and Martin, then CEO of PepsiCo UK and Ireland, were debating the future of one of Martin's most promising lieutenants at a corporate succession retreat. Both were equally unyielding in ongoing conversations about PepsiCo's future leadership.

At an impasse, neither knew where to go next. But as key executives in the C-suite, alignment between the two about the company's future direction was critical.

Roger was sure he was right about Martin's candidate, but also frustrated he hadn't been able to communicate that successfully.

Martin thought he understood Roger's objections, but he didn't buy into them. Adamant that his candidate was the right fit, he would not let the subject drop.

Martin broke the silence.

"Roger, yes, I get it—he isn't a people person," Martin said. "But everything else checks out."

Roger took a breath as he found the point he'd been waiting to make:

"Unfortunately, Martin," he said, smiling, "*people* are the only species we employ."

— — —

For Roger, intelligence that facilitated results was not enough. Instead, he saw a leader's real gift as taking people along by inspiring them to achieve purpose-driven personal and organizational success. This was one of the company's key leadership drivers. As the architect of Pepsi's successful growth strategies at the end of the twentieth century, Roger knew that leaders who elevate their people, teams, and companies can achieve something much bigger than simple, short-term objectives: they can learn to lead through anything.

Roger's observation carries even more weight now than it did then. In today's world of near-constant disruption, a slew of conflicting demands conspire to crush leaders. Internally, employees require personalized leadership tailored for different generations, cultures, and age groups. Externally, never-ending geopolitical, climate, financial, and health crises conspire to continually raise the stakes.

As lifelong students of leadership, we've observed how this chaos affects leaders: while some thrive, many others buckle under the strain. There is, unfortunately, no universal leadership handbook all managers are given when they get promoted. Instead, they're forced to navigate through an unending stream of books, social media posts, and lectures. While well-intended, much of that guidance makes it easy to get lost in the details by creating unnecessary complexity that makes it hard to understand the big picture and the true essence of leadership. This is why we've written this book: to provide the time-tested guidance that we've found sorely lacking in even the bestselling leadership titles.

As you'll learn as you progress through this book, our training as professional leadership advisors and coaches has inspired us to take a different approach. Our mission involves identifying the most promising ideas within this complex landscape. But we don't just stand outside the battle and advise. We're in the trenches with our clients. What we're sharing has been road tested, built over 40-plus years, and is constantly evolving with the largest, most complex organizations, as well as some of the smallest and fastest-growing ones in the world.

This book represents a collaboration born of our two-decade partnership as leadership advisors, colleagues across multiple firms, and personal friends. Dustin brings more than 30 years of experience advising senior executives, and Ed nearly 20. Our bond straddles two generations (Gen X and millennial) and two continents (Europe and North America). Between us, we've coached and advised hundreds of executives and C-suite teams across every industry vertical in more than 70 countries.

Today, we are partners in the London and Los Angeles offices of one of the world's top leadership advisory firms, which for many years has provided consulting services to more than 70 percent of Fortune 1000 companies around the world.

A leader's journey of growth is inherently personal, so our relationships with our clients stretch far beyond the office, corporate conference rooms, and Zoom sessions. We focus on creating trusted bonds, and in many cases, deep friendships, which we cultivate through shared experiences. We've raced kayaks with a global leadership team on Lake Mondsee in Austria, sung karaoke with energy industry executives at Orlando's Disney World, toasted to client successes with financial services leaders atop the

Park Hyatt in Tokyo, and played soccer with a global consumer business leadership team in Jeddah, Saudi Arabia.

Through the years, we've grown into members of each other's families. If one of us faces a crisis, or wants to celebrate a big win, the other gets a text, phone call, or Zoom. We haven't always worked on the same projects together, but our shared belief in the power of leadership has created an unbreakable bond that led to writing this book.

We believe the escalating challenges and crises of the modern era make exceptional leadership truly indispensable. Our lifelong commitment is to not only create a world better led today, but also to create a road map we can entrust to future generations—including our kids—that will enable them to lead through anything and build a better world long into the future.

Our objective with this book is to deliver a logical, inspirational, and simplified approach to leadership that cuts through the ever-growing noise that leaders encounter. This approach will help you improve your resilience, effectiveness, and impact. In other words, we want to help you realize your potential to become a Thriving individual and leader who shapes Thriving organizations. Our strategies are unique in that they are designed to help you continually level up your impact as an individual, manager, and leader. They're adaptable to whatever situation you find yourself in—whether that involves knitting together a diverse team of managers, coaching an underperforming employee, managing boardroom expectations, launching a new strategy, or coaxing a reluctant teenager to mow the lawn.

As you'll learn in Chapter 1, Thriving is a personal and leadership mentality that balances *purpose*, *vitality*, and *agility* to achieve sustainable success. Individual greatness—stardom—is often reachable with an imbalance, and can destabilize or diminish the impact of others around the "star" leader. In comparison, the well-balanced leaders we are highlighting not only outperform as individuals, but also make the people and organizations around them better. So that you can orient yourself most effectively with this approach, here are some helpful ideas to keep in mind.

## These Principles Represent an "All-Weather Model"—Come Rain or Shine

Let's not kid ourselves. We're in a downpour right now. It is often the case that leaders blame external circumstances or challenges outside their control, like the weather, for being a drag on their effectiveness. We specifically shaped this model to remove that variable. These principles are effective in all times and all conditions. When you work on these principles, good things can and do happen anywhere and everywhere.

No matter the external circumstances or the size of the team, business, or market, these are the principles we have found you need to focus on to inspire the highest level of performance in yourself and others. Most importantly, these principles empower you to move from being the victim of the metaphorical weather on any given day to becoming the calm center of whatever weather system the day brings you. They are your ongoing navigation system and source of power.

We asked ourselves, based on our research and combined 40-plus years of experience with C-suite leaders around the world, what would we tell every leader? The answer is that when you focus on understanding, internalizing, and experimenting with this model, you will be on the right track.

As Warren Bennis, the renowned leadership expert, once said about leadership: "Becoming a leader is synonymous with becoming yourself. It is precisely that simple, and it is also that difficult."[1]

## These Principles Are Simple, Not Simplistic

Leadership and culture are complex. Simplicity for its own sake can miss the mark. Our focus is on doing the hard yards that are necessary to get to the simplicity behind the topic. Do not be fooled by the lack of endless 10-point checklists in this book. We have grown dubious of some popular books, trainings, and social media posts that bombard you with a thousand things, terms, and approaches to hold in your increasingly limited white space. We find these approaches disingenuous in that they pitch themselves as helping you cope while simultaneously loading you with more to-dos. There is not enough time in the day!

Rest assured that we have done our best to roll these ideas up to the highest possible level to simplify your to-do list. At the same time, there is plenty of room for growth within each principle, and we have yet to find a particular trending topic with respect to leadership that cannot be contained in one of them. For instance, inclusion and belonging fit superbly within the vitality principle, as you will learn later. Some topics fit across all the principles. But the main point here is, if you can name it, we can show you how it fits into this fully comprehensive model.

## These Principles Can Be—and Have Been—Backtested for Validity

Beyond our research and modern applications with clients, we challenged ourselves to look back through history and apply these principles to standout leadership victories. From sports to politics to business and back again, they are clearly evident in individual, team, and organizational successes, big and small, no matter the industry or context. In fact, that's where many of the stories we share originate.

At the same time, you can apply the lack of one or more of these principles to leadership failures across contexts. We will explore later why all three of these dimensions must be present to maximize performance, and how to spot when you are strong in certain areas and deficient in others.

## Everyone Will Have a Strength and a Challenge Area—Yes, *Everyone*

The simple truth is that we can't all be great at everything. That includes us, and you. Throughout this book, we encourage self-reflection and self-assessment. When we do so honestly, our research has found that the vast majority of us have what we call a "front burner" principle, which is a clear strength, and "back burner" principle, which is a clear area in need of development. That is perfectly normal.

There are leaders, and then there are Thriving leaders. The leaders we're talking about have all three elements of strength in equilibrium.

None of the leaders we write about here, or work with, emerged from the womb with the perfect triumvirate of Thriving. We each, based on personal passions, talents, and circumstances, have developed strong muscles in certain areas and used them to get results that have powered our careers. The model in full gives us each something to aspire to as we scale our vision and impact to the next level.

It's important to note that even Warren Buffett, now in his nineties, encourages others to take time to invest in themselves and their leadership. As you will learn, Thriving gives us an effective road map for how to focus that investment.

## Each Principle Contains Three—or More— Dimensions to Develop

Our experience has taught us that it is not useful to think of each principle as a simple on or off switch. There are multiple levels of development within them, so each of us possesses and applies some aspect of the principles in our own way. We have taken the time to categorize three mission-critical dimensions of each principle, supported by stories and evidence, to showcase what brings them to life. The stories include leaders from a variety of industries and backgrounds to illustrate the universal application of each principle. These leaders are from South Africa, Lebanon, Turkey, France, Germany, the United Kingdom, the United States, and more. Some of these leaders we've worked directly with; others are leaders who have been retained by our firm. The final group is leaders we admire.

## It All Starts with You

What's exciting about this methodology is that it begins with you. You are the only person or factor that you can truly control. As the scope of your leadership grows, whether as an entrepreneur running your own business or the CEO of a large corporation, people increasingly look to you as a role model. We believe in the idea widely known as "Shadow of the Leader," meaning that people you lead are always aware of your presence, your energy, what you promote, and what you permit. They use these clues to shape their own thinking and behavior. Whatever you focus on tends to become the focus of others around you.

Know and appreciate the power you have at your disposal as a leader. If you take the time to start with yourself and focus on developing these principles in your mindset, attitudes, and behaviors, you will create near-magical results in a natural and authentic way. These can include:

- Aligning people and energy to a common cause
- Building incredibly effective teams and helping them work together more selflessly
- Evoking positive emotion more often in yourself and others
- Increasing engagement and retaining more of your top talent
- Speaking to the deep human need in your employees, customers, and stakeholders to belong and make a difference
- Shaping a positive, impact-driven organizational culture
- Helping everyone to demonstrate healthier values

The state of Thriving is an absolutely achievable, positive psychological state of mind, regardless of your profession or management level. When you lead from it, you create a domino effect. Your resulting higher performance and elevated mood or state of mind encourage and support a healthier, more efficient environment. And the improved organizational environment becomes more beneficial to the individual and the team. What's most exciting is that once the three core principles are understood and balanced within yourself, the integration of the state of Thriving as a lifestyle takes place naturally and automatically. All that's required from you is the desire to learn and experiment with new ideas and approaches.

The journey of this book is split roughly into thirds. The first part explores each foundational principle of the Thriving state: *purpose*, *vitality*, and *agility*. The second focuses on measuring yourself and your organization against them, understanding the power of all three together, and learning about methods that foster a Thriving state. Finally, we complete the journey by helping you understand how the principles differentiate top leaders, what the Thriving teams of today and tomorrow look like, and how to create a Thriving leadership legacy.

We're excited to share these stories, experiences, and lessons with you because we believe the world needs more and better leaders to master the escalating challenges of this new era. But as Einstein said, "We cannot solve our problems with the same thinking we used when we created them."[2] This book describes how we can collectively level up our thinking and our approaches so we can learn to lead through anything.

One final note: At the end of each chapter, we offer a set of three questions designed to process and integrate the information you've just read from insight to action. The first question is designed to prompt reflection; the second, experimentation; and the third, choice. We hope these will help you put the solutions we're offering into practice in your career and your life.

Welcome to a better way to lead.

# CHAPTER 1

# Prototype of a Thriving Leader

aking his boss's point to heart, over the following decades Martin Glenn focused on creating people-driven workplaces, right down to the front lines, wherever he led. An eventual four-time CEO, after leaving PepsiCo, where he was CEO of Walkers, Martin went on to successfully lead Birds Eye Iglo, United Biscuits, and the English Football Association (the FA). In our decades working with him through a variety of roles and organizations, we've come to appreciate his qualities as an exceptional strategic and critical thinker, innovator, and friend.

During his four-year tenure with the FA (which ended in 2019), Martin introduced a schedule revamp that created a winter break for players and adopted the NFL's "Rooney Rule" as part of an effort to increase diversity.[1] The Rooney Rule mandates that teams must interview at least one African American, Asian, Hispanic, or other minority applicant for every future managerial and executive role.[2]

Martin was credited with improving association and team corporate culture as well as football and financial performance. Both women's and men's soccer teams reached the World Cup semifinals, while the FA notched a 40 percent increase in revenue. These gains facilitated record financial investment of more than $125 million in grassroots soccer across England as well as the establishment of a national soccer training facility to develop future talent.[3]

Like other learning-oriented leaders we have coached, Martin unlocked qualities within himself that inspired durable personal and organizational success at scale. Regardless of the setting in which he found himself, the recipe for his achievements didn't change. Not many leaders possess the flexibility and vision to achieve success across such diverse businesses as consumer brands and sports governing body leadership. Martin seamlessly navigated the transition by applying people-first principles.

Martin is what we call a Thriving leader. These leaders demonstrate the ability to create a Thriving state in themselves, and shape a Thriving organizational culture that helps their businesses continually evolve and generate sustainable success. And we mean "sustainable" in the broadest sense, far beyond exceeding analysts' earnings per share (EPS) and sales expectations. Even in difficult times, leaders like these somehow defy gravity and, in spite of the odds, find a way to take flight against all opposing forces. All thanks to creating and sustaining a Thriving state.

## Understanding the Thriving State

How did the principles of the Thriving state come to light? At the beginning of the financial crisis of 2007, the global culture-shaping firm Senn Delaney (now part of Heidrick & Struggles), turned a spotlight on what separates the highest-performing leaders and organizations during times of great challenge. Initial questions that drove the exploration included:

- Is there a set of common principles that these high performers intuitively share?
- If so, can the principles be learned and understood by people and teams so that those preferred mindsets and behaviors can be shaped into the organizational norm?
- Is there a clear approach to sustaining that high-performance culture once established?

The answers were uncovered through a collaborative study with three prominent US business schools—University of Michigan's Center for Positive Organizations, the University of Southern California Marshall School of Business, and University of California Irvine's Paul Mirage School of Business. The study, conducted in December 2008, surveyed thousands of leaders and managers from more than 60 global organizations across all industries and integrated Senn Delaney research, interviews, and data from their Thriving Index Survey.

The initial research confirmed three key points, among others. First, there are indeed shared principles at play in the mindsets and behaviors of the highest performers. Second, the leaders who operate from these principles consistently perform at the top 10 percent of performance ratings. Third, 80 percent of the time, people deemed to be High Thrivers (scoring high across all three principles) automatically model the high-performance cultural behaviors that are found in the healthiest and highest-performing organizations according to the firm's Thriving Index. Simply put, High Thrivers shape healthier, higher-performing cultures around them.

A lead researcher from USC added: "Our research has shown that people in a Thriving state perform much better as rated by their managers and go above and beyond the call of duty. They do things that really benefit other members of the organization and the organization itself. The idea of being in a Thriving state, of being your best self, actually is very beneficial to those around you in the organization."

Senn Delaney's press release put a finer point on the findings: "Leaders who operate from a Thriving state and model these principles in the leadership shadow they cast over their organizations can create Thriving cultures beneath them. Mastering these three principles will lead individuals, teams and organizations to healthier, higher levels of performance."

In summary, the state of Thriving is an achievable, positive psychological state of mind, regardless of a person's profession or management level. The improved organizational environment automatically becomes more beneficial to the individual and team. In symbiotic fashion, the resulting higher performance and elevated mood (or state of mind) encourage and support a healthier, more optimal environment. Shape a Thriving culture and you'll create a self-sustaining, high-performing organization for the long haul.

Since this research was first shared with the world, we've made it our mission to positively impact the world by inspiring leaders to shape Thriving organizational cultures. Where we begin that journey with any leader is with an explanation of the three principles. Let's dive into them now, and we'll continue to share findings from the research along the way.

The study identified the three common principles that underlie this Thriving mindset in individual leaders:

- **Purpose:** Direction, clarity, and personal and professional alignment. Leaders with purpose create and share a vision that motivates collective achievements and aspirations.
- **Vitality:** A sense of connection and being absorbed in the moment, feeling energized. Leaders with vitality generate a high level of trust within their teams and organizations.
- **Agility:** Curiosity, creativity, innovation, and constant searching for knowledge and growth. Leaders with agility inspire themselves and others to learn and improve.[4]

We captured the integrated nature of these principles in Figure 1.1. The overlap of all three is what we refer to as the "sweet spot," where all cylinders of the engine are firing together. These principles provide, in a simple diagram, a road map for this book and your leadership journey.

**FIGURE 1.1 The Thriving State**

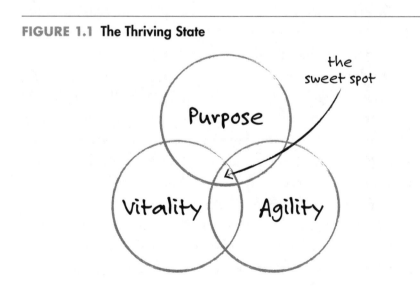

Because Thriving leaders are rare and special, it wasn't easy to decide which leader would lead off this book. Ultimately, we didn't have to look far to find her: Queen Elizabeth II, who died in September 2022 at age 96, represents Thriving at its highest state. Certainly, she wasn't perfect. But the way in which she led the monarchy and the United Kingdom through seven tumultuous decades of disruption demonstrates that she grew in her role over time to comfortably occupy the intersection of purpose, vitality, and agility in an unprecedented manner. During this period of time, the Queen led, changed, and evolved herself and the monarchy. The only way this can be accomplished is with a sense of purpose and service, a sense of connection, and a willingness to change and adapt. These are the principles that guided her over the 70 years of adaptation to an ever-changing external environment.

We've chosen one incident from her long reign to capture her unique take on Thriving.

When Queen Elizabeth II visited the Republic of Ireland in 2011, she was the first British monarch to visit Ireland since Irish independence in 1921.[5] Decades of conflict strained the relationship between Britain and its former colony to the breaking point despite an official peace treaty signed in 1998.[6]

While the fighting was officially over, the wounds were far from healed when Elizabeth undertook her historic visit.[7] Wearing green in honor of Ireland's reputation as the Emerald Isle, the Queen began her address to the country's politicians and leading citizens at Dublin Castle in Gaelic, the Irish national language.[8] The crowd gasped in surprise as a spontaneous round of applause broke out.[9] This moment was all the more remarkable because it occurred in Dublin Castle, the former headquarters of British rule in Ireland, in the Irish language, which the British had banned in an effort to suppress Irish nationalism.[10]

During this speech, Elizabeth II said: "To all those who have suffered as a consequence of our troubled past, I extend my sincere thoughts and deepest sympathy. With the benefit of historical hindsight, we can all see things which we would wish had been done differently or not at all."[11] Her speech spoke to the bond between the two countries, "the ties between our people, the shared values and the economic, business and cultural links that make us so much more than just neighbors, that make us firm friends and equal partners."[12] But she didn't stop there. The Queen laid a wreath, while bowing her head, in the Garden of Remembrance in Dublin, a park dedicated to the Irish who fought against British rule. She visited the Croke Park football stadium, a site where British-administered police in 1920 killed 14 civilians during a soccer match in reprisal for Irish Republican murders the prior evening.[13]

The *New York Times* described the visit as "a trip that ranked among the most politically freighted of her almost 60 years on the throne. While the Queen has no formal political power, her visit—the first by a British monarch—offered powerful symbols of reconciliation and drew broad acclaim among Irish politicians. Her status both as the head of state and as the most respected member of Britain's royal family was taken by her hosts as imparting a particular gravity to her words, sealing a closeness that has grown in recent years."[14]

That Elizabeth, the symbol of the British state that inflicted so much pain on the Irish, could help heal those wounds is a testament to her sense of purpose, vitality, and agility. She undertook this visit with her unwavering belief that it was her duty to nurture a closer relationship between Britain and Ireland, part of the sense of purpose that defined her 70-year reign. Her sense of agility and vitality won over skeptical Irish politicians and the public at large due to the sincerity and respect with which she delivered her spoken and unspoken messages.

Essentially, she went to Ireland to repair a broken relationship by creating connection. There's no doubt that she succeeded.

This is one story within her 70-year reign, and there are countless others that highlight the special capacities she had as a leader.

Using these principles as a lens through which to observe leaders clarifies how and why certain leaders succeed over time while others fail. These principles are fully embodied in Roger's people-centric observation, Martin's herculean career trajectory, and the sense of respect and civility with which the Queen undertook her Irish visit. Leaders who model these attributes, individually and collectively, find their success ripples exponentially across their organizations, through the executive ranks, line management, and to the frontline workforce.

Why are these three forces so critical for the most senior leaders to model? Just as a stone thrown in the middle of a pond sends ripples to the shore, CEOs leading with purpose, vitality, and agility influence their organizations to build a similar, compounding momentum. The result is a sum far greater than its parts. Leaders we have worked with have called it an "unstoppable force" that accelerates the sense of purpose and community inside the organization. From there, the results quickly follow. Additional findings from the research help explain why. Leaders who thrive at a higher level demonstrate a significantly greater sense of optimism and belief in the future, as well as balanced judgment, confidence, courage, and direction. In addition, they feel twice as stable and secure during challenging times.

"If you can be stable, secure, and optimistic in times like this, your outcomes are going to be better," reflected one of the lead researchers. "Lower-Thriving leaders are going to send their organization sideways and could cause a snowball effect that would make a bad situation worse." Instead, "Higher-Thriving leaders see the upset, even feel some of the upset. But they are thinking about where they're going to go next, how they're going to get through it. They're twice as optimistic . . . as anyone else because of their mindset." Thriving leaders generate trust and respect, task-focused accountability, and global information-sharing within their organizations, all behaviors that define the most outstanding cultures.

Another useful lens to examine these leadership principles is through the following archetypes we've identified:

- **The Struggler:** Is tossed about by the continual waves of disruption, either lurching from one priority to the next or drowning in a sea of information.
- **The Superhuman:** Attempts to bash their way through the surf despite the growing size of the waves appearing in front of them.
- **The Surfer:** Rides the waves of change, harnessing the energy of the waves while conserving their own vitality for the challenges that lie ahead.

Low-Thriving leaders typically slot into the first two categories. They tend to either go under or move into reactive mode. In considering the Struggler leader, Dustin remembers an afternoon when he was surfing off the coast of California. This happened to be an El Niño year. There he was, paddling out, paddling out, paddling out, and paddling out, and the surf kept dragging him back. This is akin to what the Struggler does—paddling out, but never achieving any forward momentum.

Leaders and organizations who fall into the second category fail in a variety of ways. One of the most common traps is juggling too many priorities. Dustin recently worked with a team whose leader boasted of managing 129 big initiatives. Unfortunately, that leader's colleagues weren't given enough direction about which priorities were the most important, so there was a constantly shifting focus that drained, rather than created, energy.

The Struggler and Superhuman leaders lack the qualities that we've identified as key to sustainable leadership. However, leaders who exhibit all of these principles—the Surfers—expend less effort and perform better by capturing the energy of change and utilizing that to transform themselves, their teams, and their organizations. Instead of being drained or depleted by continual disruption, they leverage it. In fact, they revel in it, with the filter of a child at play.

Ed recalls an executive he worked with reacting to the continuing twists and turns of the pandemic saga with sheer wonder: "Isn't it fascinating? This thing is really giving us a run for our money. We're doing all we can to stay ahead of it." No matter the continuous waves, that Surfer leader kept getting back on the board. We refer to this as a type of mental weatherproofing that involves watching the currents, seeing the patterns, adjusting, and adapting. Leaders in this case stay in the present moment, while observing trends and maintaining fidelity to their vision.

Futurist Alvin Toffler captured the urgency of the task that leaders, teams, and organizations face in this era of constant disruption: "The illiterate of the 21st century will not be those who cannot read and write, but those who cannot learn, unlearn and relearn."[15]

Thriving leaders are the Surfers who empower their people and leverage a Thriving mindset to unlock their organization's full potential, no matter the circumstances. Leaders just like the ones in the examples that follow. If you're looking for a leader that you can measure yourself against in terms of the highest levels of Thriving, pay attention to these stories. In the illustrations below, we've intentionally separated out the specific qualities of Thriving to dive into these individual qualities. All three of these leaders—Larry Merlo, Dominique Leroy, and Brian Chesky—possess all three qualities that distinguish Thriving leaders. We're placing a magnifying glass on some of their specific traits in order to clarify what Thriving means.

— — —

## Thriving Leaders Deliver on Purpose

When Larry Merlo joined CVS as a regional manager in 1990, the retailer was acquiring competitors in a drive to establish a leadership position in the nation's drugstore market. A pharmacist by training, Larry had worked his way up from a community pharmacist to a regional manager at Peoples Drug Store, which CVS acquired that year.[16]

More than 30 years later, Larry retired as the most successful CEO in CVS Health's history, after transforming the drug retailer into a holistic healthcare company.[17] The key to his success? Creating and executing a broad, clear, purpose-centered vision. Instead of fixating on dominating one sector, Larry built an integrated healthcare company through a strategic approach that included turning around its pharmacy benefit management subsidiary Caremark and acquiring insurer Aetna. This vision created a uniting purpose for Larry, his executive team, and the entire organization.

Today, CVS is a vertically integrated healthcare company dedicated to improving healthcare, building healthy communities, and innovating through healthcare technology. Throughout his tenure, Larry stood out as an executive unafraid to take risks. There were few risks bigger than his 2014 decision to stop selling tobacco products, a move that cost the company $2 billion.[18]

CVS Caremark became the first major US pharmacy chain to stop selling tobacco products, including cigarettes, in all its stores.[19] In announcing the decision, Larry characterized the move as proactive: "By eliminating the sale of cigarettes and tobacco products in our stores, we can make a difference in the health of all Americans."[20]

A few years later, the verdict on his big bet was in.

"After CVS's tobacco removal, household-and-population-level cigarette purchasing declined significantly. Private retailers can play a meaningful role in restricting access to tobacco. This highlights one approach to reducing tobacco use and improving public health," concluded a study published in the April 2017 issue of *The American Journal of Public Health*, published by the American Public Health Association.[21]

Larry's gutsy decision exemplified the qualities required in today's challenging leadership environment—perhaps the most difficult leadership environment modern executives have ever encountered. Larry realized that CVS could not build a brand as a holistic healthcare company while peddling tobacco products, so he discontinued their sale.

While there's no doubt that Larry and the company profited from his leadership and that pivotal decision, his accomplishments went far beyond corporate profits. Instead of becoming a slightly better and more profitable version of itself, CVS pursued a more expansive vision, metamorphizing into a mission-driven company dedicated to improving healthcare across America, fueled by their purpose: "Bringing our heart to every moment of your health."

The results speak for themselves. Since Larry became the heir to the CVS CEO position in 2007, the stock price of CVS has grown by a factor of 3 compared to a significantly lower growth factor for its closest competitor.

Instead of just trying to simply get bigger, Larry transformed the company into CVS Health and then in 2021 passed the baton to the next generation of leadership: Karen S. Lynch, executive vice president of CVS Health and president of Aetna. Upon the announcement of her promotion to CEO of CVS Health, which was effective February 1, 2021, Karen said, "Never has our purpose been more critical than during these unprecedented times."[22]

## Thriving Leaders Create Vitality

Another High-Thriving leader, Dominique Leroy, rebranded and reshaped Belgacom—now Proximus—15 years after the privatization of the Belgian state-owned telecom. Hired to transform the slow, underperforming organization, Dominique successfully built a nimble, vital company competitive with her peers across Europe. Prior to Dominique's tenure, Belgacom was a run-of-the-mill European telecom with a predictable suite of consumer and business services, including mobile, broadband, TV, and fixed line.

Dominique projected a return to growth within three years, a period of time that seemed reasonable to her. For many, however, that goal seemed overly ambitious. After losing market share for more than 15 years, stakeholders doubted that she could reverse stubbornly negative trends such as high customer churn, elevated customer acquisition costs, and low employee engagement.

Dominique and the Proximus leadership team clarified their goals to this: to learn, grow, and change faster than anyone else. Driven by Dominique's ability to connect, generate trust, and work effectively with a diverse set of stakeholders, Proximus exceeded Dominique's initial goals, and the company returned to growth within 18 months. By the two-year mark, Proximus achieved a number-one ranking in customer service within their markets. Not only that, but customer churn went down, and employee engagement went up, all while customers signed up at an encouragingly high rate for multiplatform relationships.

Dominique facilitated many of these accomplishments by encouraging responsibility down the corporate ladder and focusing on empowerment. Years of a top-down budgeting process had taught managers that senior leaders would pass down plans and budget from above; the managers were then expected to execute that budget, in which they had little or no input. Such a top-down budgeting process can demoralize managers because it implies a lack of knowledge and respect while also depriving these managers of any say on future priorities in their area of responsibility.

Flipping the script, Dominique gave these same managers high-level targets, allowing them to decide how to achieve those goals. While managers confessed to some angst in being handed so much responsibility, they ultimately owned the process, delivering realistic, achievable, and intelligent budgets.

Dominique's purpose-driven and inspiring style helped catalyze organization-wide change, not just at the top of each line of business, but for all employees, from managers to frontline workers. When Dominique enters a room, she immediately gains everyone's attention, not only for her energy, but also for her ability to listen closely and attend to people and the environment around her.

Speaking of her experience at Proximus, Dominique said: "Trying to create a team from a bunch of individuals was quite a challenge—getting to know each other better and trust each other more. We also had to define the common vision and a strategy that was agreed upon, shared, and which could be transparently communicated to the rest of the company. That took time, meetings, coaching, and feedback. It's not an easy process, but when you get there, it's really powerful."

With thousands of employees spread across a large geographic footprint, the CEO can't possibly impact each employee, office, or line of business on a one-to-one basis. Instead, CEOs must create a choir—so to speak—so those leaders can accelerate the dissemination of specific cultural messages.

Dominique co-created a definition of the mission-critical culture dimensions with her team and encouraged executives and managers to lead within that agreed-upon framework. In practice, this means executives and managers understand the organizational purpose, values, and key guiding behaviors and attitudes that will best enable their business strategy so they can act as one.

The foundation of Dominique's success was, and continues to be, the combination of the three qualities we consistently identify in sustainable, high-performance cultures: purpose, vitality, and a growth mindset fueled by agility.

Many leaders understand the shortcomings of their organizations and devise plans to fix them, but lacking one or more of these three characteristics, they fail to facilitate necessary and durable change. The impact of Dominique's Thriving leadership helped the organization to defy the gravity of its legacy struggles. She worked with her team to shape a leadership program called Good to Gold to encourage growth-oriented cultural practices.

"In the end," Dominique said, "we were not doing things that are very different from our competitors. We're investing, we're transforming, and we're cutting costs. But why are we so successful so far, when others are not? I think it's about the soft issues, about changing the mindset of the people. What made the difference was the Good to Gold culture. That was the glue that enabled us to bring these transformational elements together."

Spoken like a true Thriving leader.

## Thriving Leaders Demonstrate Agility

Twelve years into the meteoric rise of online hospitality marketplace Airbnb, Brian Chesky felt optimistic. A singular focus on "building a 21st-Century Company that serves all our stakeholders" based on trust, health and safety, and positive experiences was producing results. Chesky's "2020 Airbnb Update" memo revealed that the firm now offered "millions of listings in more than 220 countries and regions and over 100,000 cities," while Airbnb hosts had earned over $80 billion in revenue.[23]

In his personal reflection as CEO on the state of the company, Chesky commented: "In 2019, we made significant foundational investments to grow and support our community over the next decade and beyond." He punctuated their run of successes by adding: "In 2020, we are looking forward to supporting our Hosts and helping travelers access even more amazing places to stay and things to do."

At the height of that success, little did Brian know that in just a few months, the company would face the most challenging moment in its history—the Covid-19 pandemic. As Chesky would later share, "All of a sudden, I felt like a captain whose ship was hit by a torpedo."[24]

As part of Airbnb's data-driven and agile culture, the company had begun monitoring guest searches on their website as a prime leading indicator of future business performance. Chesky noted, "Before people book an Airbnb, they type a location and dates with long lead times." Even a casual review of the information stream at that time revealed a disturbing story. Within approximately eight weeks, Airbnb's business dropped 80 percent and, with universally halted business travel representing 50 percent of their revenues, all leading indicators went off a cliff. The company, along with the rest of the world, was plunged into crisis.

Airbnb's corporate culture dictated a belief in hard data and the hard truths that patterns in data reveal. This conviction is core to an agile, learning culture. Brian and his team weren't going to hide from the brutal facts revealed by the data.

"I have been in crises before," Chesky said. "Airbnb, in a sense, was started during my own personal crisis when I could not afford to pay rent. One of the first lessons I learned is that in a crisis, you have to move much more quickly." Before Covid could wreak further havoc, Airbnb's leadership acted decisively. Relying on their well-developed adaptability and resilience, leadership quickly engaged in a stakeholder-aligned crisis management plan that emphasized conserving cash, resizing operations, and repositioning their business model for the future. "We realized we had to get back to our roots," Chesky shared. "We had been pursuing many initiatives . . . which we had to scale back. We turned what had been the equivalent of a ten-division company into a single-division functional organization, and we had to reduce the workforce by around 25 percent."

In Chesky's widely publicized all-company memo on May 5, 2020, he announced the change in direction and layoffs. In addition to detailing a generous and far-reaching severance plan for impacted employees, Chesky underscored the need to "map all reductions to our future business strategy and the capabilities we will need." He emphasized that while it wasn't clear when travel would return, his belief was that it would ultimately look fundamentally different than it did before the crisis.[25] The great pivot and refocus of Airbnb was on.

As painful as these moves were, they paved the way for Airbnb's post-crisis rebound. Because the company stayed ahead of the curve, its strategic repositioning was implemented just as its leading indicator data reflected an increase in searches for personal stays to help people get closer to key family members.

Even more significantly, the high-performance culture that Airbnb had fostered throughout the company paid dividends. The remaining engaged workforce understood the threat the pandemic posed to the company and responded, adjusting to the change in direction.

Emerging from the initial crisis, the company benefitted from sharpening its focus. Airbnb's pivot didn't go unnoticed. Rebounding financial results later in 2020 soon put the plan of going public through an IPO back on the table. Chesky called it "the ultimate comeback story."

On December 10, 2020, less than a year after its business was body-slammed by the pandemic, Airbnb launched a successful initial public offering at $146 per share on the Nasdaq, more than doubling the initial $68 per share and valuing the company at more than $100 billion.[26] Emerging from a global disruption as an even more valuable company, especially one ravaged by the pandemic, is no small feat.

Enabled by a purpose-focused culture of 5,000 employees who pulled Airbnb forward, Brian surfed the waves of disruption, both personally and professionally. Personally, he overcame a significant test of his capacity to lead himself and others through crisis. Professionally, he helped to reposition and focus Airbnb for the long term, likening the journey to parenthood. "The company is 13 years old. You don't raise your 13-year-old to be a good 14-year-old. You raise your 13-year-old to be a great adult with a long career over many decades. That is how we're thinking about Airbnb."

Brian faced the difficult reality that the pandemic inflicted on global business, while at the same time retaining a sense of purpose, vitality, and agility that enabled the company to adjust and then, just as quickly, bounce back.

It's hard to separate Airbnb's success from Brian. Even the pandemic couldn't knock him down—although Airbnb was in a difficult period, Brian leveraged the moment to reflect on and embody leadership principles that have enabled him and others to remain calm, optimistic, and agile. Chesky later shared the personal epiphany that guided his actions: "The way a company handles a crisis is often the way the leader handles the crisis, and that comes down to the leader's psychology."

One of Brian's skills—a crucial skill of the Surfer leader—is the ability to shift his focus between the present and the future. Brian focused on riding the wave, aware of where he was while scanning the break ahead to anticipate the next move.

## Thriving in the Era of Permanent Disruption

These three successful leaders demonstrated Thriving in an era of constant disruption. As we write this, organizations and their leaders are challenged by an onslaught of factors such as activist investors, global pandemics, supply chain dislocations, raw materials inflation, rising cost of capital, financial crises, and geopolitical upheaval, not to mention AI and technological disruption.

We believe that today's—and tomorrow's—environment will resemble a metaphorical war zone of constant change and dislocation that we liken to the downward pull of gravity. There is always a force running against you and your leadership plans. If you're clinging to the hope that the geopolitical, economic, business, or public health environment will return to the "normal" we experienced earlier in the twenty-first century, it's time to drop the fantasy and acknowledge reality.

As we continue to explore these dimensions of effective leadership, you'll learn why the state of Thriving is so critical in this era of permanent disruption. We expect internal and external disruption to escalate, meaning that leaders who realize and facilitate a state of Thriving in themselves and their organizations will ride the waves of dislocation while exerting less energy and improving performance. Leaders must stay focused on the horizon, anticipate the future, and adapt rapidly—in other words, they must continually find ways to lead through anything. Thriving is *the* antidote.


## Why We Do This Work

The approach we take in coaching, facilitating, and consulting is uniquely suited to helping individuals—at any stage of their career—cultivate the critical qualities that this book will reveal. Over time, our work with CEOs, C-suite executives, and other leaders around the world has resulted in comments such as:

- "This turned around my company."
- "This transformed my team."
- "This took our business to the next level."
- "This changed my life."*
- "This saved my marriage."*

We have had the privilege of helping our clients improve by staying in their corners, asking meaningful questions, helping them find their own answers, and creating room for individual authenticity while applying these principles. These realized individuals explore what leadership means to them, so they can inspire that in others. This book is an attempt to capture the spirit and essence of these meaningful partnerships.

We will share the stories and lessons of a diverse set of the leaders we've worked with. We've also chosen to include leaders we've not had the privilege to work with because we believe they

---

* Yes, a client really said this.

are role models of the principles and results we capture in this book. Some are household names, and some you'll be hearing of for the first time, but all share the capabilities we'll illuminate here.

By design, our methodology leads to strong results for organizations, with clients reporting a range of positive outcomes, from revenue, margin, and market share growth to dramatically improved engagement and customer Net Promoter Scores to improved safety and critical operating metrics. In addition, the research shows that:

- Over 70 percent of individuals who live and learn at the top levels of the Thriving traits perform better than their peers.
- 80 percent of those with these Thriving qualities automatically model high-performance culture behaviors in their organizations.
- 70 percent of leaders who integrate and achieve a balance of the Thriving principles are predicted to succeed.

More recently, Heidrick & Struggles undertook new research to further strengthen the link between Thriving organizational cultures and company financial performance. Through a survey of 500 CEOs from around the world and across industries, they found that a small, elite group—called "Culture Accelerators"—who put shaping a Thriving culture first enjoy double the revenue growth of others (9.1 percent CAGR vs. 4.4 percent). These findings were summarized in a 2021 report called "Aligning Culture with the Bottom Line: How Companies Can Accelerate Progress."[27]

The exciting news is that individuals, teams, and organizations that achieve the Thriving state foster a culture of leadership excellence from the top to the front lines that sustains over time. Over the next several chapters, we'll guide you through an in-depth exploration of each of these principles. You'll learn why each of them is significant in itself, what happens when one of the three is missing, and why our hands-on experiences have proven that they are so powerful in concert.

This leadership guide offers you a blueprint to help you bridge the gap between where you are today and the leader you can be tomorrow. After more than a decade of research, our own collaborations, and consistent hands-on application with clients, we are ready to help the world lead through anything.

## From Insight to Action

**Reflect:** How are you feeling as a leader today? Are you a Struggler, attempting to be Superhuman, or feeling balanced as the Surfer? Why?

**Experiment:** Plan an upcoming day as an "awareness experiment." Notice opportunities to apply the three attributes of Thriving. What did you learn?

**Choose:** Write down the "why" for improving your leadership capacities. Why is now the time to grow?

## PART 2

# THE ANATOMY
# OF THRIVING

# CHAPTER 2

# The Power of Purpose

For nearly 100 years, the South African company Telkom played a dominant role in the country's communications infrastructure. A legally sanctioned government monopoly, Telkom thrived because it controlled all communications.

However, in 2005, that advantage began to erode as the government authorized competition and courts allowed internet service providers to build and operate their own networks. Telkom experienced self-inflicted wounds due to failed acquisitions and a lack of visibility into the expanding mobile phone market.[1] More nimble competition chipped away at Telkom's markets, leaving the company in a defensive, reactive position.

When Sipho Maseko ascended to the CEO position at Telkom in April 2013, he faced an enormous challenge. In addition to eroding market share and declining profits, its largest market, South Africa, was struggling economically. The administration of President Jacob Zuma, elected in 2009, was wracked by scandals.[2] While the economy and middle class grew significantly in the post-apartheid era, inequality, poverty, and unemployment continued to plague the country.[3]

As a leader with a demonstrated track record of vision and purpose, Sipho viewed his task at Telkom through the wider lens of South African—and African—prosperity. His vision was to transform Telkom into a premier provider of communications services and infrastructure to attract inbound economic investment to South Africa and the entire continent. By democratizing access to technology, Sipho hoped to facilitate individual and business communications, e-commerce and critical healthcare, and educational and business services.[4] Not only did Sipho possess a sense of purpose for Telkom that was larger than himself, but he also tied the company's future to the future of the country and the entire continent. That's the purpose component of Thriving writ large.

To accomplish this task, his first job was to resuscitate Telkom with financial discipline and cultural reinvention. At a breakfast meeting one morning, Dustin was struck by Sipho's commitment to changing the company's culture. After describing strategies to create cultural change, Dustin listened as Sipho queried him on a deeper level, asking, "What if I want to shift the spirit and soul of my organization so that I can bring hope? How do I do that?"

As a leader in a country and continent with a legacy of conquest by the West, with fragile social, political, and economic structures, Sipho was well aware of the challenges ahead of him, his company, his country, and his continent. But he didn't let that deter him. Seeking to magnify his impact, he placed purpose at the center of his cultural reboot of Telkom, inspiring his executive leaders, managers, and frontline employees.

In developing countries like South Africa, there are a host of obstacles that inhibit critically needed inbound investment, including an unreliable electrical grid, water shortages, and insufficient infrastructure. Telkom couldn't tackle all of those issues, but the company could leverage its resources to create a reliable telecommunications infrastructure.

Defining this purpose created a road map for Sipho to transform Telkom from a traditional telecommunications company to one pursuing a vision of a connected country and continent. During his tenure, Sipho changed the focus of Telkom from that of a fixed-line provider to a mobile provider, while increasing mobile subscribers by a factor of 10, decreasing dependence on the fading fixed-line business, and increasing revenue by more than 30 percent.[5]

In this chapter, we'll share more of Sipho's journey and how it embraces the three central aspects of purpose: the Human Compass, the Horizon Hunter, and the Committed Servant. And you'll meet several other exceptional leaders through whom we'll explore these three characteristics in more depth.

## THRIVING PRINCIPLE #1

**PURPOSE:** Direction, clarity; personal and professional alignment. Leaders with purpose create and share a vision that motivates collective achievements and aspirations. (See Figure 2.1.)

**FIGURE 2.1 The Principle of Purpose as Part of the Thriving State**

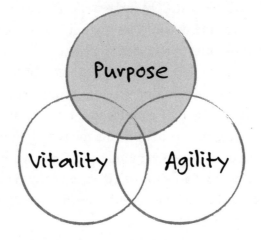

*"The two most important days in
your life are the day you are born
and the day you find out why."*
—MARK TWAIN

*"Efforts and courage are nothing
without purpose and direction."*
—JOHN F. KENNEDY

## How Purpose Works

Purpose is the first of the three key principles associated with the highest-performing individuals, leaders, teams, and organizations. In conjunction with vitality and agility, purpose allows CEOs to create and sustain organizational excellence. In this chapter, you'll learn more about how the most effective leaders and organizations demonstrate the three essential facets of purpose. We offer three examples of the specific facets below so you can understand how they function in practice.

For purpose to be truly effective, it must be clearly articulated, authentic for the people and organization, and embraced by all levels of leadership.

When Thriving leaders approach the development of a unifying purpose statement, work usually begins with a collective definition of the organization's reason for being at the highest level. Once the direction is clarified, consistent communication is required to spread and reinforce that purpose throughout the organization and customer markets. For the power of purpose to be fully expressed, it can't be mere words in a company annual report. Instead, purpose must be leveraged as the central platform that informs organizational strategies and decisions, so that it's truly felt by those who work and interact with the company.

When that happens, leaders can generate and maintain trust in the North Star of the organization and in each other's intentions. Trust leads to confidence, which creates the space for leaders to implement purpose-based strategies and decisions for the organization's managers and workers to execute. Research findings note that purpose isn't necessarily confined to individual or organizational goals; instead, purpose can exceed these boundaries, evolving into societal and global visions, like in Sipho's case.[6]

Purpose-driven leaders and organizations leverage this clarity to improve performance. A positive purpose inspires upbeat energy and emotions, countering the negative effects of gravity. When executives, managers, and frontline workers demonstrate belief in the organization's direction, their collective energy is aligned toward a common goal.

In today's tumultuous environment, a collective purpose speaks to the human desire to make a difference. Purpose-derived values enhance culture and create a healthy collaborative environment. Finally, organizations with a strong sense of purpose increase employee engagement and retain talent for the long haul because employees often report feeling part of something greater than themselves and empowered to make a difference.

As the late General Colin Powell said, "Perpetual optimism is a force multiplier."[7]

## The Three Facets of Purpose

Leaders can exemplify the principle of purpose through three distinct archetypes we'll explore here:

1. **The Human Compass:** Articulates a clearly defined purpose and direction, which they employ to keep their teams on track and impact the world around them.
2. **The Horizon Hunter:** Maintains focus and anticipates the impact of the converging streams in the distance that will shape the future.
3. **The Committed Servant:** Seeks impact derived from their sense of purpose, striving to positively impact their customers, employees, stakeholders, communities, and world through service.

Sipho, as CEO of Telkom, exemplifies all three. His work to define the company's direction resulted in a clear, forthright mission statement: "Telkom's purpose is to seamlessly connect our customers to a better life."[8] The company's strategy elevates that purpose: "We are playing a leading role in South Africa's digital revolution by leveraging our converged ICT leadership to enable solutions that enrich our customers' lives, be it at work, through online education, or via entertainment."[9]

The Horizon Hunter characteristic involves bringing the future into the present. In other words, Horizon Hunters work to differentiate between trends that will stick and those that will fade. In seeking to create a truly diversified information and communications technologies (ICT) provider to enable South African and African consumers and organizations to prosper, Sipho fulfills the criteria of a Horizon Hunter. Today, Telkom operates in 38 out of the 54 countries on the African continent.[10]

To accomplish this goal, Sipho added the mobile component neglected by his predecessors, moving Telkom from ranking dead last in South African mobile providers to third (of five).[11] Going far beyond mobile, Telkom's business units cover every facet of modern communications and technology infrastructure.[12]

To further realize their collective vision for a truly modern and revitalized South African economy, Telkom supports small and medium-sized enterprises through the company's Diverse Supply Chains and Sales Value Chain programs, which are designed to offer opportunities for business within Telkom's supply chain while mitigating supply chain risks. To fill its talent pipeline, Telkom funds a coding curriculum and school-based problem-solving and understanding value curriculums.

Through addressing the needs of South African and African consumer and business customers for information and communications technologies, Telkom seeks to fulfill its purpose to connect its customers to a better life.

## The Human Compass

While the AIDS epidemic is largely in the rearview mirror in many Western countries, the same can't be said for Africa. More than two-thirds of the 34 million HIV-positive people in the world live in sub-Saharan Africa. That translates to nearly 24 million HIV-positive people in Africa. More than one million adults and children die of HIV/AIDs in Africa each year, while 91 percent of the world's HIV-positive children live in Africa.[13]

For Tommy Clark, a Dartmouth College and Medical School graduate, these tragic facts became all too real for him as an English teacher and a member of the Zimbabwe football club the Highlanders. "People I knew—teammates, fellow teachers—were dying of HIV, and nobody talked about it," he said. Tommy immediately began to wonder if football could help build HIV/AIDS knowledge and awareness in Zimbabwe.[14]

His early experiences there inspired him to become a pediatrician after graduating from medical school. During his residency, he gained the support of his residency director to found Grassroots Soccer.[15] The organization's approach is based on social learning theory, which was pioneered by Stanford University psychology professor Albert Bandura. A chance meeting between Tommy and Albert convinced Tommy of the validity of this theory, which states that behavior can most effectively be changed through the use of role models.

Grassroots Soccer was founded on the premise that leveraging popular, respected, and successful soccer players as role models can build "confidence and resilience in young people so that they can take control of their lives and health, on the field and off."[16]

Founded in 2002, the nonprofit initially relied on small donations from friends and other individuals.[17] Today, supported by partners such as the Bill and Melinda Gates Foundation, Nike, and the U.S. Agency for International Development, Grassroots Soccer operates in 45 countries. Leveraging the power of soccer, the organization helps over a million youth by educating, inspiring, and mobilizing them to overcome health challenges such as HIV/AIDs, as well as confronting mental health, gender violence, and teenage pregnancy.[18] By 2028, GRS has plans to positively impact the lives of over 10 million adolescents in Africa and around the world.

Grassroots Soccer isn't just about changing the lives of adolescents in Africa. It's also about employing evidence-based approaches and replicating its model for a sustainable solution to the challenge of empowering the youth of the globe's most impoverished continent. As a true Human Compass, Tommy has maintained the power of his purpose to propel Grassroots Soccer from its modest beginnings to the success it enjoys today. Tommy's compass is changing the health, welfare, and trajectory of African youth. The Human Compass never loses sight of their ultimate purpose.

## The Horizon Hunter

For Mark A. Gabriel, personal and organizational purpose must be forward-focused. As the former CEO of the Western Area Power Administration (WAPA), he is a lifelong professional in the utility industry. Mark understands the need to move toward a sustainable energy future. He's the author of *Visions for a Sustainable Energy Future*, published by Routledge in 2008, a book designed to help energy professionals, corporate executives, investment professionals, strategic planners, and regulators navigate the rapidly evolving, competitive energy environment.[19]

Mark left WAPA after delivering on their multiyear road map to become the CEO of United Power, an electricity cooperative based in Colorado. In his first message to the co-op's 300,000 members, he captured the challenges and promises facing the industry:

> We are witnessing a huge transition in the most critical commodity of our lives. The shift toward low or no carbon generation, the expansion of beneficial electrification and the development of innovative technologies generate engaging conversations with members and are driving some

*of the greatest changes we have seen in society in the past 75 years.*[20]

Like a true Thriving leader, Mark demonstrates foresight and the ability to articulate a bold vision in purposeful yet practical terms. He works diligently on his communications to achieve this impact. When leaders internalize what they see on the horizon and use that vision to inform the context of their messages on a consistent basis, they exponentially increase the sense of urgency and impact felt by their audiences.

Another Horizon Hunter leader we've worked with focuses on long-term strategies built out over 5, 10, and even 20 years. These strategies are purpose-driven to ensure the company brand remains relevant far beyond the lifespan of its current leadership.

To stay anchored in this long-term perspective, the leader habitually creates time and space to consider crucial questions such as:

- Where's the world going?
- How do we remain relevant?
- How do we best serve our communities and regions?
- How can we best benefit our customers?
- How can we ensure we're still making a positive difference in 10 or 20 years?

This focus has implications for all employees, from top leadership to the front lines, and compounds the benefits of long-term thinking from today far into the future.

## The Committed Servant

When Paul Polman unveiled a plan in 2010 to double Unilever's revenues while at the same time cutting its negative environmental impact in half, his ambitions seemed contradictory. Doubling a consumer goods company's sales meant consuming more electricity and using more natural resources, which would make it that much harder to achieve his environmental goals.[22] But Paul was committed to a new capitalism that embraced all stakeholders and prioritized the environment.[23]

Through his Unilever Sustainable Living Plan, his objective was to "set some big—uncomfortable—targets to keep us focused," said the former CEO, who retired in 2018. Paul believes that sustainability belongs at the center of corporate purpose and strategy. "Businesses thrive when they serve all their stakeholders: citizens, employees, suppliers, partners, those who make up the extended value chain," he remarked. "When you make your business relevant to the needs of the communities and societies you serve, then everyone benefits, including shareholders."[24]

Under Paul's stewardship, Unilever nurtured more than 25 purpose-led brands, including Seventh Generation, Schmidt's Naturals, and Tazo Tea. In 2018, these sustainable living brands grew 69 percent faster than the rest of the company's businesses, a significant increase over the 46 percent growth rate in 2017. In fact, seven of the organization's top ten brands were identified as sustainable living brands, which are those "that communicate a strong environmental or social purpose, with products that contribute to achieving the company's ambitions of halving its environmental footprint and increasing its positive social impact."[25]

During Paul's 10 years as Unilever CEO, the organization delivered consistent top- and bottom-line growth, ultimately recording a 300 percent shareholder return.[26] When he retired, he founded Imagine, a consulting company, and wrote a book called *Net Positive: How Courageous Companies Thrive by Giving More Than They Take*.[27]

We've worked with many executives who are inspired by service. One memorable leader is Umran Beba, former chief diversity and engagement officer at PepsiCo. This was her final role at PepsiCo, after a long and successful career as a P&L leader and then HR leader. She's delivered top-quartile engagement and performance results, and in her final P&L role, achieved this despite a tsunami, extreme flooding, fires, and a major earthquake in her region. Her commitment to diversity drove exceptionally high employee engagement results and rapid growth in her divisions as she ascended the corporate ladder in Turkey, the eastern Mediterranean, and finally, the Asia-Pacific region (APAC).

She reached the zenith of her career at PepsiCo when she was promoted to the top organizational position in diversity and engagement. Her experience in this position drove her belief that diversity "gives us a competitive advantage and can drive innovation and growth. As an international producer of consumer goods, foods, and beverages, our customer base is very diverse. It is of vital importance that this base is represented in our workforce."[28]

PepsiCo tasked Umran with achieving its Performance with Purpose 2025 agenda, which includes achieving gender parity in management roles by 2025. This approach is designed to achieve these goals across all 200+ countries and territories where PepsiCo operates.[29] Umran and PepsiCo are living the service aspect of purpose actively.

## From Purpose to Vitality

We've demonstrated how purpose is a critical attribute for leaders and organizations that seek to thrive amid constant disruption. Leaders who demonstrate one or more of the archetypes of the

Human Compass, Horizon Hunter, and Committed Servant inspire their organizations to create a better world.

In Chapter 3, we move on to the mindset of vitality, which is a characteristic that displays positive energy, connection, and inclusion. Just as purpose is a necessary quality in the healthiest and highest-performing teams, the cohesive power of vitality ensures that leaders and organizations stay enthusiastic, resilient, and connected on the path toward fulfilling their purpose.

## From Insight to Action

**Reflect:** Which of the three purpose archetypes— the Human Compass, the Horizon Hunter, or the Committed Servant—is most like you at this moment? What's a recent example of how you demonstrated this capability?

**Experiment:** Pick one archetype you'd like to explore or improve. What upcoming opportunities do you have (e.g., critical meetings, project deadlines, public appearances) to experiment with a new approach? What action will you take?

**Choose:** What outcomes do you want to see in yourself and in others as a result of improving the dimension of purpose?

# CHAPTER 3

# The Power of Vitality

Unlike some professional athletic coaches, cutthroat competition never solely defined Phil Jackson's approach to basketball. Instead, Phil, an 11-time U.S. National Basketball Association (NBA) championship coach, relied on awareness, connection, and presence to transform the ordinary into the extraordinary.[1]

Phil employed a strategy that emphasized vitality and relationships in contrast to the authoritarian techniques utilized by many coaches. Across 20 seasons as a coach—and 12 as a player for the New York Knicks and New Jersey Nets—Phil collected a record-breaking total of 13 championship rings with the New York Knicks, Chicago Bulls, and Los Angeles Lakers.[2]

Describing his approach in an interview with the Buddhist magazine *Tricycle* in 1994, he said, "It's a warrior attitude—without having to be violent. When I came into the NBA as a coach five years ago, basketball was all about power—who had the biggest guys, who played the roughest games, who could intimidate who. Our system moves away from that. The whole concept is to defy pressure, to work against the other team's force. Basically, we try to get the other team to overload in one area and then work with their energy."[3]

Central to Phil's strategy is connection and the concept of the team as one unit, rather than a collection of individuals. "We also use the idea of a circle," he said. "The circle is a spiritual symbol for the Native Americans because it encompasses all of life—the unity that is all one. We stand in a circle when we meet on court; we bring everyone into the group. The basketball is a circle; the hoop is a circle. These are symbols or reminders that the circle is one. We talk about things that open up the players' minds and bring them ideas from other cultures to help them develop as a team."[4]

Phil's approach was successful in uniting diverse groups of highly talented individuals with vastly different backgrounds, experiences, and attitudes. One of his players, Lamar Odom, captured Phil's attitude in the wake of a midseason five-out-of-eight losing streak by the Los Angeles Lakers in 2011. He described this experience in the *New York Times*:

> *So, Lamar Odom was asked in a grave tone, what did Jackson say to the team?*
>
> *A tongue lashing?*
>
> *A flogging?*
>
> *"What time is the bus?" Odom said, smiling.*
>
> *That minimalist message was Jackson's way of saying, "When you guys are tired of this, let me know."*

*If the instinct of many coaches would be to tighten the screws, Jackson often loosened them. If this allowed for stretches of ambivalence in the regular season, it also allowed his teams—not just the stars—to navigate the emotional caldron of playoff basketball in a cool, trusting manner.*[5]

Not only were the playoffs stressful, but the regular season could be a trial as well, given the personalities involved. Notable members of the Bulls and the Lakers during his tenure included Michael Jordan, Scottie Pippen, Dennis Rodman, Shaquille O'Neal, and Kobe Bryant.[6] Jackson, a master of vitality and connection, blended these stars and dozens of other players into cohesive units that thrived, season after season. Clearly, Phil's approach to NBA coaching embodied the principle of vitality.

In this chapter, we'll highlight some additional elements of Phil's approach that speak to vitality. You'll also be introduced to other extraordinary leaders who epitomize the three core attributes of vitality: the Energy Multiplier, the Inclusion Advocate, and the Clarity Creator.

## THRIVING PRINCIPLE #2: VITALITY

**VITALITY:** A sense of connection, being absorbed in the moment, feeling energized. Leaders with vitality generate a high level of trust within their teams and organizations. (See Figure 3.1.)

**FIGURE 3.1** The Principle of Vitality as Part of the Thriving State

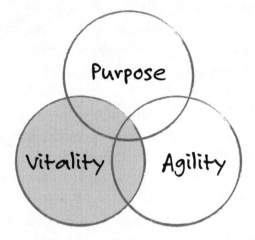

*"Emotion eats reason for breakfast."*
**—TIM LEBERECHT**

*"We are not a team because we work together.
We are a team because we trust, respect,
and care for each other."*
**—VALA AFSHAR**

## Thriving Through Vitality

Vitality is the second of the three Thriving principles necessary for sustainable, outstanding leadership, both personally and organizationally. Leaders can exemplify this characteristic through three distinct archetypes:

1. **The Energy Multiplier:** Generates, builds, and focuses energy, starting with his or her own, to accomplish personal and organizational purposes.

2. **The Inclusion Advocate:** Notices, appreciates, and celebrates the unique gifts and greatness of all individuals, harnessing that power for the collective good. Fosters a sense of belonging across organizational boundaries.
3. **The Clarity Creator:** Defines and enforces personal and organizational boundaries to focus efforts on what is most essential at any given moment. Creates priorities while declining commitment to noncore strategies, tasks, and objectives.

While there are many leaders who excel in the principle of vitality, Phil is an outstanding representative of this attribute because he so clearly exemplifies the three main archetypes. Phil has the most NBA championships of any coach, exceeding legendary Boston Celtics coach Red Auerbach by two.[7]

Throughout his coaching career, Phil demonstrated the ability to repeatedly generate, build, and focus energy. His energy wasn't loud—instead, it was systematic and consistent, motivating groups of different professional basketball players to win 11 championships over 20 years. A year after taking over as head coach for the Chicago Bulls, Phil melded a disparate group of players into a team that won three consecutive NBA titles from 1991 to 1993. Two years later, he did it again when the Bulls captured NBA titles from 1996–1998. Leaving Chicago for Los Angeles, Phil won three more consecutive championships from 2000 to 2002, and two more in 2009 and 2010.[8]

Such a feat has never been accomplished by another professional coach in any American professional league. In American football, Bill Belichick of the NFL New England Patriots came close, with six championships between 2002 and 2019.[9] In baseball, Yankees manager Joe McCarthy won seven World Series rings in the 1930s and 1940s.[10] In hockey, Toe Blake won eight

Stanley Cups as the coach of the Montreal Canadiens during the 1950s and 1960s.[11]

Phil leveraged the power of inclusion by helping his players consider their impact on others more fully. This was a skillful way to reach his players, who although they were some of the most talented players to ever play the game, were not always the most sensitive or aware individuals. He described his approach to Michael Jordan in his book, *Eleven Rings: The Soul of Success*:

> *I didn't dictate to him what I wanted; I simply pushed him to think about the problem in a different way, mostly by asking him questions about the impact that this strategy might have on the team. "How do you think Scottie or Horace would feel if you did this?" I would say. I treated him like a partner, and slowly he began to shift his way of thinking. When I let him solve the problem himself, he was more likely to buy into the solution and not repeat the same counterproductive behavior in the future.*[12]

As the Clarity Creator, Phil incorporated some lessons into his coaching that he learned as a player. Realizing that getting too amped up before or during a game led to less concentration rather than more, he established ongoing mindfulness practices such as meditation. "I discovered playing for the Knicks that when I got too excited mentally, it had a negative effect on my ability to stay focused under pressure," he wrote in *Eleven Rings*. "So, I did the opposite. Instead of charging players up, I developed a number of strategies to help them quiet their minds and build awareness so they could go into battle poised and in control."[13]

## Saad Abdul Latif: The Energy Multiplier

The energy of a Thriving leader is not to be confused with mere charisma. This is especially true when it comes to the Energy

Multiplier archetype of vitality. While charisma is a fleeting, unsustainable quality, vitality is not. Instead, when a leader with vitality enters the room, the place lights up due to the sense of authentic connection and belonging that the leader fosters. In other words, when you're in the presence of a leader who is an Energy Multiplier, you feel a sense of psychological safety. You're energized, loyal, and willing to go the extra mile for that person. Through our leader relationships, we've come to realize this dynamic is not by chance. Leaders intentionally nurture their own energy so they can be present and connect more meaningfully with others. It is a choice.

One leader who embodied that attribute was Saad Abdul Latif, who was the CEO of PepsiCo Asia, Middle East, and Africa until he passed away in 2013.[14] The first time Dustin met Saad, they had dinner at a restaurant on the banks of the Nile River in Egypt. Dustin immediately launched into a spiel about what he hoped to accomplish during their consulting engagement, which would start the next day.

"No, no, no," Saad said. "Let's enjoy the evening. Look at where we are."

Putting work aside, Dustin and Saad engaged in an extraordinary six-hour conversation, which covered topics including their families, their values, their stories, and their backgrounds. The interaction was a pure human-to-human connection.

At the end of the evening, Saad sat back, smiled, and said, "You know what? This is right. We're going to be great together. Let's meet tomorrow morning and talk about what we're doing and where we're going."

For Saad, it was all about connection. Every time Dustin saw Saad over the next dozen years they worked together, Saad would immediately bound over and give him a big hug. What stood out to Dustin about Saad was that the vitality inherent in Saad brought out the same in Dustin.

And it wasn't just Dustin. Throughout the PepsiCo AMEA region, Saad treated everyone, regardless of their position, with the same warmth, energy, and appreciation. As a result of Saad's ability to generate and multiply energy, his division consistently achieved more than it forecasted. Dustin remembers a critical meeting between Saad and the bottlers in the region who were responsible for distributing Pepsi beverages. The bottlers' agenda didn't always align with PepsiCo's agenda.

Even though the bottlers weren't pleased about what they were being asked to do, Saad sat down with them, connected with them, and listened to them. Saad attended to conversations at what we call the highest level of listening—listening with full presence. At the end of the meeting with the bottlers, Saad had addressed their concerns and energized them to the point where they bought into the possibility and picture of the future that he saw—because they saw it together. Ultimately, it was Saad's ability to connect with the bottlers and listen to them that convinced them to follow a new direction.

## Krishnan Rajagopalan: The Inclusion Advocate

Building a sense of belonging is critical for leaders and individuals who want to tap into the vitality aspect of Thriving. Krishnan Rajagopalan, CEO of Heidrick & Struggles, has created a far different firm than it was when he took over in July 2017. His dedication to a culture of inclusion has resulted in a firm that has brought in multiple individuals with the different perspectives that those with different backgrounds, genders, and ethnicities bring.

Under his leadership, Heidrick pledged that at least half of the board candidates presented to clients over the course of a year will be diverse. Two of the firm's core partnerships are with Paradigm for Parity and the 30% Club's Future Female Directors program, both of which are designed to achieve more gender parity on corporate boards.

The pandemic, which was a destabilizing time for many organizations, brought Krishnan's power of inclusion to the fore. His brand of leadership created a sense of oneness, connection, belonging, harmony, care, and empathy—to all executives, managers, and employees working remotely across the globe. By the time the pandemic began to wind down, the organization was truly collaborative.

Krishnan also possesses the ability to remain focused on the present moment. When talking with him, his complete and absolute attention is focused on you. In a world rife with distraction, that's very powerful. Heidrick is now a bigger, better, more complete organization than it has ever been in its 70-plus years.

## Nick Neuhausel: The Connector

Another example of this superpower is Nick Neuhausel, a former CHRO and Chief Administrative Officer in the energy industry, senior partner for a leadership consulting firm, and mentor of Ed's. Regardless of the client or the client's circumstances, Nick always finds a positive way to establish, build, and maintain personal connections.

Many years ago, Ed found himself struggling with the new consulting firm he had joined, wondering if he really did fit in with his team. In their few interactions, Ed always sensed Nick brought laser focus to building up those around him, so Ed reached out, in hopes that Nick would offer a fresh and useful perspective. Less than 12 hours later, Ed received a heartfelt reply to his email that read, in part: "Ed, thank you so much for sharing this with me. I had no idea of your struggles. I would love to talk about what's going on for you because I really believe that this is the right place for you."

During that conversation, Nick attended to Ed in a way that left him feeling heard and appreciated while helping him renew his focus and commitment. That interaction became the first of countless others over the years. In fact, they have created an ongoing relationship so meaningful to Ed that his son's middle name is Nicholas.

Outside of their personal connection, Ed witnessed Nick's talent for employing the power of inclusion with clients who seemed so difficult and unpleasant that Ed couldn't help but wonder why they were even working with them. But Nick would always remind him to assume positive intent, to presume a basis of goodwill, and to work to see the best possibilities for others. This attitude had the potential to transform what might have been an unpleasant and difficult relationship into a genuine collaboration beneficial to both parties.

One of Nick's best-known quotes underscores the wisdom he brings to inclusion and culture that transcends context and organization: "A key measure of a company's cultural health is how you treat people when they join, and how you treat them when they leave." Even when people choose to leave Nick's teams, he wishes them well, stays in touch, and cheers them on. That mentality inspires the kind of loyalty that is impossible to replicate without authenticity and intention.

## John Clayton: Diversity Champion

The late John Clayton, a former colleague and leadership consultant, stands out as an exemplary listener and executive coach. Regardless of who he encountered, John effortlessly established a sense of inclusion and connection with that person. Not only did he create a versatile, talented team of coaches and support staff, he recognized the unique attributes of all of his clients, prospective clients, and stakeholders.

John's gift for the power of inclusion was a key building block in creating a diverse team. Diversity unlocks possibilities. Diverse individuals contribute different talents, viewpoints, and experience to a team, building a powerful dynamic that allows them to outperform more static, less diverse teams. At its best, the power of inclusion manifests for everyone, regardless of their status within the organization or their performance. In short, people always felt a sense of belonging with John. In fact, John would make a special effort to reach out to anyone he sensed was struggling and invite them to his house. Those individuals inevitably left John's house feeling an improved connection to him and the team. In most cases, that translated into improved performance.

John's ability to look beyond himself—or, as he put it, "get over himself"—created space for others to capitalize on their gifts and talents in an expansive way. This was effective both internally and externally. Dustin remembers a time when he and John were driving to meet with a difficult client. We've all had them—someone who can be quite challenging to work with. On the drive, John counseled Dustin to sit quietly while he talked to the client and to think about what he appreciated about that person. "What do they bring that you couldn't do? What do they do well? What's special about them?" he asked Dustin.

Dustin recalls how John's patience and power of inclusion transformed what could have been an extremely awkward and unpleasant meeting into one where they were able to create some common ground with the difficult client, improving their working relationship and creating a positive basis to move forward. In the years that he worked with John, Dustin learned how to capture and share vitality and the power of inclusion, skills that have enhanced both his professional and personal life.

## Bart Becht: The Clarity Creator

While the first two archetypes of vitality focus on the connection created between individuals and teams, the third focuses on the nature of the work they perform together.

Bart Becht, who became CEO of Reckitt Benckiser after it was created via a merger in 1999, possessed a special gift as a Clarity Creator who could determine and then enforce a laser focus on the company's core priorities to the exclusion of other distractions. All too often, leaders and organizations get tripped up by a lack of prioritization, which ultimately causes them to spread investments of effort, time, and money too broadly, leading to a complete squandering of the organization's valuable energy.

Bart's talent for clearing the field led Reckitt Benckiser, a global consumer products company, to focus on what it termed power brands, its 18 leading brands, including Lysol, Air Wick, and Strepsils, a sore throat treatment. As the company either developed or acquired a power brand, it reinvested 12 to 13 percent of its revenues in product marketing and brand innovation, specifically on those top brands.[15] In contrast, its competitors tended to spread their marketing dollars over their entire product lineup, according to a case study by Harvard Business School.[16]

These power brands were also in higher margin and higher category growth areas, which meant that the company reaped more rewards from its innovation and investment.[17] "It's very simple," said Bart. "Why do we focus on 18 power brands and not on the other brands? For a very simple reason—growth is much higher in the power brands because they are in high-growth categories where we have strong positions—it's no more complicated than that. . . . It's not because we don't like the other brands, but we are not going to invest as much in those brands as compared to the bigger growth opportunities."[18] In essence, Bart has a great gift for removing distraction and complexity, unlocking the energy in people and the organization through simplicity and clarity.

An unrelenting focus on attaining above-average industry growth, high profit margins, and strong cash flow allowed the company to leverage its leading brands into innovation designed to continue to drive growth forward, Bart noted in 2007.[19] Understanding that it could not do everything, the company focused its efforts on realizing innovation based on input from customers, suppliers, managers, and employees versus actual R&D spending.[20]

Instead of engaging in expensive campaigns to develop, launch, and market new brands, the company innovated within its existing brands to achieve incremental gains which, over time, added up. "I like to compare innovation to baseball," Bart said. "People think that it's all about hitting home runs—it's not. Innovation is about getting many base hits and occasionally hitting the home run. You rarely win a baseball game just by hitting home runs. And the objective is to win the game."[21]

## Vitality Brings It All Together

Ultimately, vitality is one of the three legs of the Thriving stool because the constituent parts empower leaders, teams, and organizations to create a virtuous cycle of focus, connection, and inspiration. There's a critical difference in this context between inspiration and motivation. Motivation involves distributing your own energy out to others so that they can accomplish whatever it is they need to accomplish. Ultimately, overreliance on motivation can turn leaders into Sisyphus, who was doomed to repeatedly roll a rock up a steep hill, only to have it roll back down.[22] Motivation in this sense is unsustainable, as the motivator will end up burning out, leaving the motivated without their catalyst.

No wonder CEOs and C-suite leaders are exhausted. They've spent decades of their lives attempting to push thousands of people. Instead of empowering your team to find their own solutions, like Phil Jackson, you're letting them over-rely on you. That means they can't find their own way, ultimately limiting their effectiveness to their connection with you and the organization. If that connection is frayed in any way, their motivation—and the drive of the entire company—is threatened. Many leaders walk a much more fragile line than they realize, which is why sustainable success is so difficult.

In contrast, inspiration breathes life into others so they can find and sustain their own fire. When vitality and connection allow space for organizations, teams, and individuals to find their own flame, collective inspiration is the result. Instead of feeling like you have to move the boulder of your organization forward every day, imagine what it would be like to have that same force pulling *you* forward. It is possible—and vitality is the key engine cylinder to power you there.

That's a talent that Saad brought to his teams, ensuring that everyone felt heard and included in collaborative decision-making processes. Nick and John attended to that loner in us all, the sense that we don't belong or are difficult. By leading with compassion, they ensured that the people they worked with felt respected and energized in moving forward. Bart ensured that his team remained laser focused on the factors that differentiated Reckitt Benckiser and kept the company's top brands outperforming their competitors year after year.

Another terrific example of vitality channeled into effectiveness and results is David Novak, who built Yum! Brands into a global powerhouse by generating, transmitting, and distributing positive energy in an inspirational way. A key principle behind Yum!'s success was the idea that everyone's job was to serve the customer. If you serve the customer, you therefore serve your team and your organization. Inverting the usual organizational chart, David believed that the best organizations embodied an upside-down pyramid.

To bring this spirit to life, one of David's key leadership habits relied on the power of recognition—ensuring that leaders, managers, and employees were recognized for their accomplishments. At Yum! Brands, recognition wasn't universal or random. Instead, the organization recognized the customer-focused behaviors that would create sustainably high performance in their restaurants, such as teamwork and positive energy. "We recognized the behaviors that we knew would get great performance in our restaurants," David said. "So when we saw those behaviors, everybody recognized them. And guess what, everybody did more of it."[23]

Novak also underscored the value in recognition to help people do more of the F-word in business: have fun! "Recognition is a wonderful way to really create a lot of fun in your company as well," he said. "You want to take the business seriously, but you don't want to take yourself too seriously. And by having fun recognizing people and celebrating other people's success, we were able to get great results."

The ability to foster energy and connection through the organization clearly was one of David's superpowers, and all the Yum! stakeholders reaped the benefits of it. Between 1999 and 2016, Yum! Brand's market capitalization grew by a factor of eight, from $4 billion to $32 billion.[24] "If you're one person getting big things done, that's pretty good, but it will only take you so far," said Novak. "If you can help a whole team or organization full of people to reach big goals, then there's no telling what you can accomplish together."[25]

Creating vitality is not just about how you interact with people, but how you shape their environment in a way that unlocks their energy and potential. David's leadership at YUM clearly demonstrated this superpower.

Now that we've explored more about vitality and why it's such a critical aspect of Thriving, in Chapter 4 we'll turn to the final leg of the stool: agility.

## From Insight to Action

**Reflect:** Which of the three archetypes—the Energy Multiplier, the Inclusion Advocate, or the Clarity Creator—is most like you at this moment? What's a recent example of how you demonstrated this capability?

**Experiment:** Pick one archetype you'd like to explore or improve. What upcoming opportunities do you have (e.g., critical meetings, project deadlines, public appearances) to experiment with a new approach? What action will you take?

**Choose:** What outcomes do you want to see in yourself and in others as a result of improving the dimension of vitality?

# CHAPTER 4

# The Power of Agility

**W**hen Steve Ballmer succeeded founder Bill Gates as Microsoft's CEO, the company was nearing the peak of its initial technology ascendence. Through the domination of American desktops and fed by the dot-com technology boom, the company's market capitalization hit $642 billion just nine months later, in September 2000. It would take 12 years for another company—Microsoft's rival, Apple—to eclipse that mark.[1]

Steve had reason for confidence in Microsoft's dominance of the technology landscape at the time, given that Microsoft released its most successful version of Windows—Windows XP—on October 25, 2001.[2]

At the turn of the twenty-first century, desktop computers were coming into their own. In fact, purchasing a PC with the latest version of Windows preinstalled was a coming-of-technology-age ritual for millions of Americans.[3] Windows XP represented a major leap forward for Microsoft in terms of system stability and user design.[4] By 2015, more than 14 years after Windows XP was introduced, it was estimated that more than 400 million copies had been sold.[5] By 2017, the operating system was still the third most popular in the world, despite the fact that Microsoft ended security support on April 8, 2014.[6]

The organization's 2000 annual report demonstrates how critical this duo was to the company's revenue and income picture: 42 percent of the company's revenue and 54 percent of its income were derived from Windows, while 46 percent of its revenue and 46 percent of its income came from apps such as Office.[7]

However, as the decade that Windows XP dominated continued, Microsoft's innovation engine slowed down. Windows mobile, the Zune music device, and the Surface tablet underperformed at a time when Apple and Google were launching and refining their mobile operating systems and mobile devices.[8] Not only that, but Windows XP's successor system, Vista, undermined their reputation in PC operating systems. Vista lacked compatibility with existing software and hardware in an era where corporate IT departments and consumers were less and less willing to pay for a new operating system.[9] It also wasn't as functional, efficient, or effective as its predecessor.[10]

A challenging reality became evident at a board meeting in January 2013 when Steve shared his vision for the company's future.

John Thompson, Microsoft's lead director, summarized his feedback at the time by saying simply, "We're in suspended animation."[11] Just seven months after the meeting, Steve announced his intention to retire. He had been instrumental in creating Microsoft's dominance and recognized that a new leader would be better positioned to take the company to its next horizon. He related his thoughts on his transition to the *Wall Street Journal*:

"'As much as I love everything about what I'm doing,' he says, 'the best way for Microsoft to enter a new era is a new leader.'"[12]

Steve's transition ultimately led to the promotion of Microsoft's Server and Tools Division chief Satya Nadella to CEO in February 2014.[13] Satya's ascendance to CEO resulted in a remarkable run of success for Microsoft, as its market capitalization has increased by a factor of nine as of this writing.[14]

Clearly, Satya represents how essential agility is in moving organizations forward. We can say with confidence that while some leaders of large companies represent the old-school leadership that has difficulty adapting to new situations, Satya embraces and handles change with ease, as evidenced by Microsoft's performance and growth since he took over as CEO.

As a leader with a flexible, growth mindset, Satya thinks in a circular, evolutionary way. Rather than relying on one or two products or services to maintain Microsoft's relevance, Microsoft has instead built businesses that align with global market trends in its cloud computing, productivity, collaboration, and gaming businesses. As an example, Azure, the company's cloud computing business, has gained significant market share at the expense of Amazon Web Services, the dominant cloud computing provider. In 2017, Microsoft had a 20 percent share while Amazon had a 65 percent share. Reuters reports that as of 2020, Microsoft increased its market share in this arena by 50 percent to 30 percent of the overall market.[15]

Agility is the aspect of the Thriving triumvirate that powers invention. In this chapter, we'll explore more of how Satya's unique set of talents allowed Microsoft to reinvent itself as a technology powerhouse.

Digging deeply into agility, you'll learn more about leaders who reflect the three core aspects of agility: the Nimble Scientist, the Reflective Thinker, and the Insatiable Voyager. Martin Glenn, whom you met in the Introduction, captures the aspect of agility that is the Nimble Scientist. Sipho Maseko, whom you met in Chapter 2, is a superb example of the Reflective Thinker. Finally, you'll reconnect with Mark A. Gabriel, CEO of United Power, another Reflective Thinker, and meet Sir Alex Ferguson, an Insatiable Voyager.

## THRIVING PRINCIPLE #3

**AGILITY:** Curiosity, creativity, innovation, searching for knowledge and growth. Leaders with agility inspire themselves and others to learn and improve. (See Figure 4.1.)

**FIGURE 4.1** The Principle of Agility as Part of the Thriving State

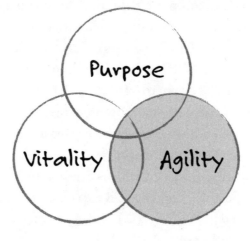

*"I never lose. I either win or I learn."*
**—NELSON MANDELA**

*"If you dislike change, you're going to
dislike irrelevance even more."*
**—GENERAL ERIC SHINSEKI**

## Deep Dive into Agility

As one of our three core leadership principles, agility is both a mindset and a skill set. Leaders can exemplify this characteristic through three distinct archetypes:

- **The Nimble Scientist:** Agile leaders believe in logic and hard evidence. In pursuit of the best and most convincing evidence, they admit what they don't know and seek knowledge from a wide variety of sources. They are curious, open-minded, and quick to embrace and test new ideas.
- **The Reflective Thinker:** At its core, this aspect focuses on deep reflection, which involves the ability to look inward in a critical way. Leaders who demonstrate this quality display foresight, which means they respond, rather than react, in solving complex problems. They integrate ideas in a playful way and balance the needs of today and tomorrow.
- **The Insatiable Voyager:** Perseverance and tenacity characterize agile leaders, who possess the ability to recognize and rebound positively and energetically from challenges and failures. These resilient leaders maintain the self-discipline and emotional focus to understand that success is a journey rather than an event.

Satya's first email to Microsoft employees as CEO reflected a new era for the company: "I fundamentally believe that if you are not learning new things, you stop doing great and useful things. So family, curiosity and hunger for knowledge all define me."[16]

Interestingly, Satya's capacity to be agile is fueled in part by learning, through his personal experiences, how to look at things differently, and being more empathetic.

Satya opened up in an interview about how the birth of his son Zain in 1996 changed his perspective and helped him become a far more empathetic person. Zain, who suffered from severe disabilities, including cerebral palsy, passed away on March 1, 2022.[17] He was the oldest of Satya and his wife Anu's three children.

"For a long time it was all about, 'Hey, why did it happen to me? Why did it happen to us?'" Satya said. "And then eventually I realized that nothing happened to me, it was my son who needed the help. And I needed to show up as a father and in some sense do my job and do my duty—but more importantly, see the world through his eyes."[18]

While it might seem like these lessons aren't particularly applicable to life as a corporate executive, he has found them immensely relevant. In fact, it is his belief that empathy is the most critical skill necessary for leading a business. Satya uses agility and empathy as methods to establish presence, read situations better, and adjust his approach to maintain forward momentum.

"Our job is to build things that somehow are in tune with these unmet, unarticulated needs of customers," he said. "It is not written down. It is not like I can interview five customers and figure it out. We say everything is automated, but you can't A/B test your way. What is the next hypothesis you are going to test? That, to me, is a form of empathy."[19]

A self-aware, introspective leader, Satya embraces learning, resilience, and reflection. In an interview with *Stanford Business*, he said, "If there's criticism for what you're doing, it's appropriate to look in the mirror and understand whether there are changes needed. Large organizations should welcome such scrutiny. We need to think about unintended consequences of our technology, for example. It's a time for self-reflection and change."[20]

Since Satya took over as CEO in February 2014 through the end of the second quarter of 2023 (when this book went to press), Microsoft's share price has increased by over 800 percent, reflecting the growth, innovation, and underlying profit that is the new Microsoft. Across a number of performance dimensions, the organization often handily meets or exceeds Wall Street analysts' estimates.[21]

## The Nimble Scientist

Leaders who think like scientists combine the ability to reason in a logical manner with a questioning mindset. While these two approaches are highly complementary, they aren't often found together. That's because a linear mind frequently turns rigid, while a curious mind is often quite freewheeling. But in Martin Glenn's case, these attributes worked perfectly in sync to deliver extraordinary results in organization after organization.

Martin's makeover of Walkers, a British snack food company where he rose from marketing manager to CEO in the course of a 14-year career, brought the company to a leading position within the UK and Irish snack market. A unit of Pepsi, Walkers combined with Smith's, a smaller UK snack brand. Under Martin, Walkers not only shed its history of uninspiring advertising, but it also created a finely tuned research machine. Led by Martin, the organization engaged in research to:

- Find gaps in their product line
- Determine customers' unfulfilled needs
- Build improved manufacturing processes
- Increase the taste and appeal of products

During his tenure with Walkers, the company reached a 45 percent share of the £2 billion 2005 salty snacks market. However, as the British public grew more obese, Martin had to contend with accusations that he peddled junk food to an increasingly overweight market.[22] Originally, Walkers launched a low-fat chip brand, Walkers Lites, in 1996.[23] In an effort to appeal to children, they launched the Potato Heads brand, which was designed for children resistant to the light brand concept.[24]

"We have a low oil production process which can take 30 percent of the oil off," he said. "We sold that as Walkers Lites for a few years and they did really well. But if you show kids Walkers Lites, they will run a mile because they think they are going to taste awful. Mums said, 'I wish you'd market stuff to me that would help me get my kids to eat low-fat stuff.'"[25]

The brand capitalized on Walkers' highly successful marketing campaign employing famous UK football star Gary Lineker emphasizing the health advantages of Potato Head chips. "Big brands stay relevant by being helpful," says Martin. "It's actually aimed at mums. The kids are quite smart: they know they don't have to use a bargaining chip with mum to get a Potato Head."[26]

Martin's background in marketing led to a revolutionary change in Walkers' approach to advertising. Scrapping the idea of a duck as the brand mascot, they instead affiliated with Lineker, one of the biggest football stars of the time. "Once the ad eventually ran, the switchboard was jammed with callers wanting to know when it would be on next. It made tabloid headlines, drew 23 complaints (not upheld) to the Independent Television Commission, but also created a wave of enthusiasm," according to CampaignLiveUK.[27]

The triumph with Walkers' marketing was just one of Martin's success stories. Under his leadership, PepsiCo's Doritos brand was launched in the United Kingdom, quadrupling the size of the UK tortilla chip market within three months and winning awards for national advertising campaigns.[28]

Throughout Martin's career, his scientific approach to business ensured that an idea or hypothesis was tested, feedback was incorporated, and results verified before the product or strategy was unveiled to the market. By engaging in a proven iterative approach to product development, Martin ensured that the vast majority of his initiatives were a success when actually judged by the market. Martin's ability to combine disparate talents such as raw intelligence, deep research, a willingness to be wrong, and iterative learning has led to success in a wide variety of leadership roles. And he's not done yet.

## The Reflective Thinker

When it comes to reflection, Sipho Maseko, the former CEO of South Africa Telekom we introduced earlier, is extraordinary. At a breakfast meeting where we delved deeply into the purpose of the organization, Sipho talked about his desire to transform the telecommunications space for South Africa and southern Africa as a whole. From the business perspective, that involved optimizing existing operations, potential internal reorganization, and acquisitions. Beyond that, Sipho went even deeper, to the point where he reflected on the spirit of his organization and where he wanted to take it in the future.

"We've talked about behaviors, we've talked about mindsets, we've talked about thoughts, but isn't there another level, the spirit or soul of an organization?" Sipho remarked. From the depths of that reflection came insights that would inform his approach to leading the organization to a better future. Ultimately, Sipho successfully communicated and executed his vision, passing a reinvigorated organization over to his successor in 2022.

"He leaves Telkom in mid-2022 with a sterling record of having delivered successive profits and a dividend to the government [the other significant shareholder]—over and above billions of taxes—with a clear and credible succession plan: a rare feat for a state-owned enterprise these days, which are a slaughterhouse for black talent," observed Sandile Zungu and John Dludlu in *Sowetan Live*, an English-language South African daily.[29] Sipho discovered and nurtured the next generation, and the source was deep reflection on the needs of Telkom beyond his tenure.

Another leader who embodies reflection is Mark A. Gabriel, introduced earlier in this book, now CEO of United Power, a rural electric cooperative serving 300,000 members in a 900-square-mile territory in the north central range of the Colorado Rockies. After Gabriel came on board as CEO in 2021, he instituted the process of formulating a 10-year plan, beginning with an eight-week period of reflection to determine the organization's priorities.

Mark's determination is pushing the cooperative into long-term planning that it never engaged in previously. He sees his role as helping his team reflect and see things that they haven't seen before, especially since the power market is evolving rapidly in response to climate change and other external factors.

As a thought leader in the energy industry, Mark is committed to helping build an energy grid that meets the needs of America today and tomorrow. In a briefing by the Environmental and

Energy Study Institute on "Modernizing America's Transmission Network," Mark wrote: "A broad and deep energy market that spans time zones and weather conditions must be built." He recommended that new technology funding should prioritize benefits for the entire country, including grid cyber-defense security, advanced sensing, and wildfire-fighting technology. In addition, he supports rectifying the growing energy divide and creating an offshore wind regional transmission organization to coordinate offshore wind planning, trading, and management.[30]

Mark's holistic view of the energy industry and his ingrained habits of reflection are helping to bridge the gap for himself, his organization, and his industry between where they are today and where they should be in the future. The Reflective Thinker must connect that aspirational future to the here and now in a way that is immediately relevant to their colleagues. Then the executive team and organization as a whole can move forward, anchored in the present and proceeding toward tomorrow.

## The Insatiable Voyager

Leaders are tested in failure much more than in success. However, there are leaders who learn from failure and never allow themselves to rest on their laurels in periods of success. They continually reinvent and grow.

When a leader takes over an organization that has ceased to believe in itself, there's a huge hill to climb to transform that mindset. Few have done it like Sir Alex Ferguson, the former coach of the Manchester United Football Club. When Sir Alex took over at Manchester United in 1986, the team was in danger of relegation to a lower division after failing to win a title for 19 years.[31] His first step was to establish a foundation for the club's future by reshaping the youth program and recruiting

more scouts. The result? That focus led to the golden generation of Scholes, Giggs, and Neville, and the signing of phenom
David Beckham at age 16 as an apprentice.[32] Together, Sir Alex
and a mix of mature footballers and new talent took Manchester United to six Premier League titles, two FA Cups, and the
Champions League over the 11 years that David was with the
club.[33]

David wasn't the only successful young recruit. Others
include Ryan Giggs, who went on to become the most decorated
British football star of all time.[34] Ryan enjoyed a playing career
of more than 20 years, ending his career in 2016 as the first
player-manager with the club since 1927.[35] His focus on players and recruitment reflected Sir Alex's belief that success was a
journey rather than a specific event.

"From the moment I got to Manchester United, I thought of
only one thing: building a football club," he told *Harvard Business Review*. "I wanted to build right from the bottom. That was
in order to create fluency and a continuity of supply to the first
team. With this approach, the players all grow up together, producing a bond that, in turn, creates spirit."[36]

"Winning a game is only a short-term gain—you can lose
the next game," he continued. "Building a club brings stability
and consistency. You don't ever want to take your eyes off the
first team, but our youth development efforts ended up leading
to our many successes in the 1990s and early 2000s."[37]

In that same spirit, Sir Alex demonstrated insight into the
iterative process that success over a long period of time requires.
He knew that organizations go through cycles and that successfully riding those waves would produce better results in the long
run. In evaluating his record in 2012, Harvard Business School
professor Anita Elberse noted, "Our analysis of a decade's
worth of player transfer data revealed Ferguson to be a uniquely
effective 'portfolio manager of talent.' He is strategic, rational,

and systematic. In the past decade, during which Manchester United won the English league five times, the club spent less on incoming transfers than its rivals Chelsea, Manchester City, and Liverpool did."[38]

To achieve this goal, Sir Alex created three tiers of players and sought to optimize the mix of those players for success within a specific cycle. "We identified three levels of players: those 30 and older, those roughly 23 to 30, and the younger ones coming in. The idea was that the younger players were developing and would meet the standards that the older ones had set." With a long-term perspective, he was able to maximize talent. "The goal was to evolve gradually, moving older players out and younger players in," he said.[39]

Sir Alex's eye for detail spoke to his tenacity. In the 1990s, the team chose gray as the main color for their away uniforms, a choice that Gail Stephenson, a vision scientist at the University of Liverpool, believed undercut the ability of the players to see each other on their field.[40] In response, the team hired her as a part-time consultant while introducing vision exercises that were designed to enhance the player's peripheral vision on the field.[41]

There's no doubt that Sir Alex's ability to pivot and reinvent his football club time and time again served the organization well. Through his years as a football coach, he won 49 trophies, including 13 Premier League titles—more than any other team in the Premier League.[42]

## The Case for Agility

To create sustainable success, agility makes the difference between "here today, gone tomorrow" and "here to stay." Leaders, teams, and organizations that make space for learning, reflection, and resilience are more likely to overcome obstacles consistently and effectively than those that don't.

We started the chapter with Satya Nadella. He's the embodiment of the Nimble Scientist, the Reflective Thinker, and the Insatiable Voyager. We will continue to highlight examples from his Herculean rise because we find him to be the epitome of a Thriving leader in many ways.

This concludes our initial deep dive into the three characteristics of Thriving: purpose, vitality, and agility. In Chapter 5, we'll examine the differences in style and outcomes that occur as leaders and organizations lead from different aspects of this leadership triad. Then later, we'll explore the power of all three at work.

## From Insight to Action

**Reflect:** Which of the three Agility archetypes—
the Nimble Scientist, the Reflective Thinker, or the
Insatiable Voyager—is most like you at the moment?
What's a recent example of how you demonstrated this
capability?

**Experiment:** Pick one archetype you'd like to explore
or improve. What upcoming opportunities (e.g., critical
meetings, project deadlines, public appearances) do
you have to experiment with a new approach? What
action will you take?

**Choose:** What outcomes do you want to see in yourself
and in others as a result of improving the dimension of
agility?

# CHAPTER 5

# Almost Thriving, but Not Quite

When Howard Schultz purchased Starbucks in 1987, the world didn't know what was coming. Howard saw an opportunity to "bring the Italian coffeehouse tradition to America" by creating a third place between work and home, where a customer could experience human connection and community while enjoying a level of quality in coffee that wasn't being offered elsewhere. Schultz's intuition was right and Starbucks took off.

The company quickly developed into a standout example of Thriving in action. Informed by its powerful founding purpose, Starbucks led the way with innovative thinking in everything from how coffee was sourced from around the world, to the layout and feel of its stores, to how it treated its employees—known famously as "partners" in the Starbucks lexicon—by offering health coverage to full- and part-time workers and stock options, known as Bean Stock. The Starbucks story took hold and their purpose expanded rapidly to many parts of the globe.

A successful IPO followed in 1992, and Schultz remained on as Founder and CEO through 2000.[1]

In our language, during this period Starbucks was the living embodiment of purpose, created incredible vitality and connection throughout the business and with customers, and demonstrated high levels of agility, implementing industry-shaping innovations. The very model of a Thriving organization.

As successful as Starbucks was, during the years following Schultz's shift from CEO to Chairman something in its magic fundamentally changed. In early February 2007, Schultz became worried the company was losing connection to its founding values. He wrote a memo to senior leadership, taking responsibility for a series of decisions that turned the company focus too heavily on economies of scale, commoditization, and efficiency at the expense of the magical customer experience and tradition that emanated from their purpose.

"We desperately need to look in the mirror and realize it's time to get back to the core and make the changes necessary to evoke the heritage, the tradition, and the passion that we all have for the true Starbucks experience," he wrote.[2]

The slowly building financial crisis in the economy and increasing attacks from innovative competitors created a difficult context for the company. In a short time, Starbucks moved from 300 percent growth over 15 years (from 1987 to 2002) to having to close almost 1,000 stores and seeing a 28 percent decrease in profit.[3]

During this difficult phase, Schultz stepped back in as CEO with a simple message on his first day: "The company must shift its focus away from bureaucracy and back to its customers."[4] Schultz knew it was time for a re-founding and transformation of Starbucks.

The company had lost something, and that something had to be restored in a way that was relevant to the fast-changing global context. In Thriving language, Starbucks' relentless focus on scale and efficiency had diminished its powers of agility, which in turn dragged against its spirit of purpose and vitality, both with colleagues and customers. It was still Starbucks, but now "not quite" Thriving.

Schultz started the transformation with a focus on leadership. At a March 2008 conference of company leaders, he presented a transformation plan that highlighted seven "Big Moves":

1. Be the undisputed coffee authority.
2. Engage and inspire our partners.
3. Ignite the emotional attachment with our customers.
4. Expand our global presence—while making each store the heart of a local neighborhood.
5. Be a leader in ethical sourcing and environmental impact.
6. Create innovative growth platforms worthy of our coffee.
7. Deliver a sustainable economic model.[5]

But, as columnist Julia Hanna writes, that wasn't enough. She captures Schultz's intention behind his next moves to inspire the Starbucks reboot:

*"I needed an unfiltered venue for expressing my empathy about all that we were asking our partners to do and telling them plainly what was at stake," he wrote in Onward: How Starbucks Fought for Its Life without Losing Its Soul. The answer, in Schultz's mind, was a three-day conference in New Orleans in October 2008, a moment when the global economy happened to be tanking. Starbucks' fourth quarter profits were down 97% from the same time a year earlier; for the fiscal year,*

*net earnings were down 53% to $316 million. The Starbucks board was reluctant to send 10,000 partners to New Orleans at a cost of $30 million, but Schultz stuck to his guns.[6]*

The revitalization and path back to Thriving had begun. Schultz outlined a clear new purpose, "To inspire and nurture the human spirit—one person, one cup and one neighborhood at a time," and unleashed the energy of the organization to make their purpose, and improved performance, the new story of Starbucks.[7]

The full details of its formidable rebound after Schultz's return are well chronicled. And we believe the continued nurturing of Starbucks' Thriving core, through the company's many ups and downs, is what established the foundation for it to remain an enduring and iconic company.

In the last three chapters, we've described the three qualities that embody the Thriving leader: purpose, vitality, and agility. These characteristics, when working together, elevate the good into the great, and the effective into the exceptional.

The goal of this chapter is to help you gain more understanding of the archetypes that dwell in the land of "not quite there" so you can assess your own situation. You'll read the stories of leaders we've previously introduced who pushed themselves beyond their comfort zones to achieve a state of Thriving. Understanding how these leaders exercise different muscles to rise above their challenges is crucial to gaining deeper insight into the Thriving model.

## Not Quite There

If you've reached the senior level of your organization, or any management position, you've obviously got a lot going for you.

The good news is that you probably have some elements of all three of the qualities that we've been discussing.

Based on our experience, it's likely that you naturally lead with one of these characteristics as a strong standout. For Dustin, that attribute is purpose—it is his natural front-burner quality that drives everything he does. Ed's primary driver is agility fueled by an insatiable learning mindset. Virtually all leaders have at least one of these qualities that is well developed; some have two of them. Rarely do you encounter a leader that runs on all three without intention.

We're not saying this to discourage you—quite the contrary. In fact, we've seen leaders who initially demonstrated one or two of these qualities develop into the most extraordinary Thriving leaders with all three in place. This book is made up of their stories. If they can learn how to nurture qualities that don't come as naturally to them, you can too. Since these characteristics can be learned and developed over time, there's the potential for you, your team, and your organization to grow into leaders who can make a powerful and sustainable difference in this world of constant disruption.

In our research, we've identified the "almost but not quite" personas, as shown in Figure 5.1. In other words, we've quantified how those who demonstrate strong evidence of two principles, but not all three, lead and where their leadership may ultimately fall short.

- **The Evangelist:** Strong on purpose and vitality; low on agility
- **The Explorer:** Strong on purpose and agility; low on vitality
- **The Brainstormer:** Strong on vitality and agility; low on purpose

When we share these personas in coaching and in presentations, we get a lot of nods and agreement. That's because these personas are quite familiar to anyone with experience in a business or organizational environment. Let's explore them in detail.

FIGURE 5.1  **Exploring the "Almost but Not Quite" Thriving Archetypes**

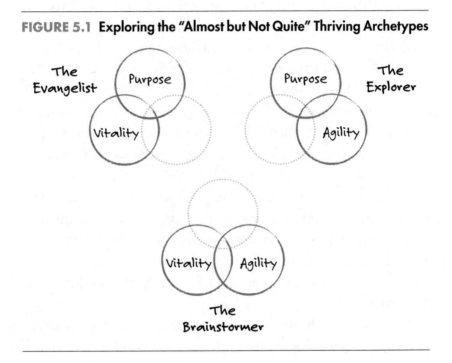

## The Evangelist

Consider the Evangelist, who tends to create an organization composed of good soldiers who follow the ideas the leader transmits and who thrive on the sense of purpose and vitality they inspire. This leader and organization ultimately run into problems, however, because the workforce has been taught not to question the ideas and edicts that come from above, but just to follow them. This dynamic tends to work for a certain period of time as the organization moves forward based on its initial purpose and sense of connectedness around that purpose. However, when the world starts to change, disrupting that purpose and vitality, these organizations typically run off what we call a cliff of irrelevance.

Because the Evangelist leader and the Evangelist-driven organization lack agility, learning, and innovation, they get stuck doing the things they've always done in a way that the rest of the world moves on from over time. Because the innovation piece is missing, the organization doesn't have the muscle to adjust to the different expectations of customers and markets. This leads to an attempt to press harder with the old methods, which creates a hamster-on-the-wheel dynamic.

A few years ago, Dustin was talking to a large European organization about helping revitalize their culture and plan for leadership succession. He and his team went in and did an assessment, looking at each of the leaders' strengths and challenges in an effort to determine who was ready to take over the organization's leadership. Unfortunately, no one was because all of the vice presidents and managers were good soldiers.

When we talked to the CEO, he was bewildered, saying, "Well, we're not sure why that happens. All decisions come up to us, so we make them and distribute the answers." Apparently, this had been going on for years. Guess what happened when the organization tried to change this approach, pushing the decision-making down to the lower levels? The vice presidents and managers absolutely hated it because they didn't want to make decisions. They'd been taught to execute, and they were very good at it. What's more, their organization was able to perform well based on their sense of urgency and can-do spirit—at least for a while. But because the innovation muscle had atrophied, at a time when there was an appetite for new ideas, there were none.

Although the organization had run, and run well, for 60 years based on purpose and vitality, they were lacking in growth and innovation. When the world needed them the most, they were not ready, willing, or able to innovate and adapt to serve it. That left the field open to their competitors, who were already taking the cake.

Within that kind of organization, it's very likely that at least some of the vice presidents, middle managers, and frontline employees wonder whether top management can actually see waves of change or competitors coming, or if they are just complacent. This can lead to the widespread belief that top leaders don't care about what's missing.

## The Explorer

Consider the Explorer, who demonstrates real strengths in purpose and agility. That creates an organization with focus, direction, and the speed to get there, while adjusting for new situations and circumstances. In this case, the team is the expedition force, following the organizational purpose to achieve great things.

The Explorer profile is seen often in early-phase tech startups, but we've seen it across industries and company sizes. After years of success built on the metaphorical equivalent of all-nighters and chugging energy drinks and coffee, these organizations tend to run into a wall of burnout. There's a point at which everyone's exhausted because there's a lack of cohesive energy and even collaboration, which is exactly why so many companies fail to progress at a certain point in their growth journey. Without a sense of vitality and collaboration, organizations are impossible to scale, which means the whole thing can just run out of gas and collapse.

Ed worked with a pre-revenue, publicly traded pharmaceutical company that exhibited extremely high levels of purpose and agility. It grew from 50 to 400 employees quite rapidly. But it began to stumble while scaling the business because there was no clear sense of cohesion, collaboration, and pulling in the same direction. Individually, the team members performed well, but the sum ended up being less than the parts because there was a lack of focused energy, with even senior team members stuck in the silos of building their own functions while ignoring their fellow colleagues. Until they repaired that gap, they were not going to be able to move forward to create the type of success their IPO had initially envisioned.

Within an Explorer organization, many wonder whether top management cares about the burnout and the lack of connection or trust. This type of dynamic is corrosive and can eat away at the organization's heart, causing infighting and talent hemorrhaging as people seek a stronger-knit community to be part of, which leaves behind a deflated, disengaged workforce that ultimately doesn't succeed in fulfilling the organization's goals. In a similar way to the Evangelist, members of these organizations wonder if their leaders realize what's missing.

There are many ways in which living through the Covid-19 pandemic felt like being part of an expedition force attached to an Explorer. Our purpose as a society was to move through it with all the energy we could muster, bobbing and weaving past the torrent of changing contexts and new, urgent information each day. But after a while, because many lacked a sense of cohesion and connection, leaders and teams ended up stuck in silos, feeling burned out and disconnected.

There was a time when you could not scan your news feed without seeing many articles highlighting stories of worker exhaustion and fatigue. Some companies successfully dialed up their energy and vitality in response, driving care and connection during the pandemic, but in many cases, it was purely temporary and dissipated as the crisis waned. Once the external impetus is gone, companies often revert to their base pattern. This notion of "reversion to the mean" is an important observation that holds true for most leaders, teams, and organizations in the absence of an external rallying cry or consistent, thoughtful leadership.

## The Brainstormer

Consider the Brainstormer, who exhibits high levels of agility and energy. These leaders thrive on collaboration and innovation, bringing in employees who love being part of an "idea convention." This atmosphere can be energizing and exciting, full of endless possibilities. The feeling at the beginning is that the sky is the limit in terms of new products, new services, and new ways of doing things. However, without the forward focus of purpose, projects are proposed and approved but never actually finished.

The "idea convention" loves new stuff but eventually sputters when the trajectory of the organization does not truly change. Eventually, people vote with their feet because even though they might hear the right messages from their leaders, they find that they are on a slow boat to nowhere.

Dustin worked with a large professional services firm with a demonstrated track record of success. It never had any problem attracting bright managers and workers, most of whom initially loved the energy and ideas. However, the firm began experiencing continual waves of attrition from employees who reported that while they loved the atmosphere, the lack of forward progress was so frustrating that it ultimately drove them out. This is where the lack of purpose can really undermine an organization, because without that uniting purpose, significant forward progress is unsustainable.

At a certain point, the same dynamic at play in the Evangelist and Explorer organizations turns up here, as more of the managers and workforce wonder what's missing and whether those at the top know what they need to do, or even care. A sense of futility can take hold where there's an ongoing vacuum of purpose.

## Taking Stock of Your Situation

You may wonder where you fit on this spectrum. It takes some time and effort to figure out your default. There may be a standout type for you and your organization, or you might see evidence across a few of these descriptions. Most important is to consider what your strengths are in the current moment, and which of these Thriving dimensions are more challenging and might hinder sustainable progress.

Once you have discovered where you are most challenged, you need to make a conscious effort to be aware of that rut, and identify methods to adjust and steer in a healthier direction. This must be done with awareness and intention because, left unchecked, we all tend to fall back into our natural comfort zones.

For Ed, his default is the Explorer role. He can easily get charged up by a sense of possibility and purpose, and immediately absorb large amounts of information to create and execute a path filled with scenarios and opportunities to get there. But if he's not careful, he can overlook the need to ensure a spirit of unity in his team, bringing others along, and establishing a healthy work-life balance. Therefore, he's highly aware that the Explorer role tends to be his natural come-from, and intentionally works on developing his muscle to foster positive energy and vitality on his teams and with his clients.

Remember, leaders who are well developed in all three areas are rare; virtually all of us have plenty of work to do. The good news is that it is entirely possible and within the realm of your capabilities to do so. But without a high level of self-awareness, reflection, and discipline, becoming a Thriving leader will always feel just a bit out of reach.

There also may come a point at which a company founder who identifies as an Explorer, for example, needs to either develop the people-focused vitality muscles or replace themselves. Otherwise, the company tends to keep looking for the next horizon, yet conquering that horizon alone doesn't add as much value as scaling the current platform through a greater sense of connection and vitality. This dynamic occurs frequently. A leader can take an organization to a certain place, but for more growth to occur, the leader either needs to add to their toolbelt of capabilities or allow for a different leader to come in and create a more sustainable path forward.

Armed with this new context, let's revisit the story of Starbucks and how other organizations completed the Thriving puzzle.

## The Evolution of Starbucks

Before Schultz returned to the CEO role in 2008, Starbucks had, in our view, demonstrated behaviors of an Evangelist organization. The relentless pursuit of efficiency and optimization delivered predictable performance for a while but eventually chipped away at the company's collective ability to adapt to the changing competitive situation and find ways to bring its unique purpose to the world without commoditizing itself. That loss of agility begins to eat away at the foundations of purpose and vitality. Before you know it, one weak leg can bring down the whole stool.

Schultz's diagnosis of the condition and treatment plan proved accurate. During his second act, Starbucks grew from just over $10 billion in annual revenue to more than $25 billion.[8] His investment in the business and its fundamentals, along with comparable investments in its people and culture, set Starbucks up for its next phase.

The lesson of their journey is clear. Without attention and intention, every Thriving organization is one decision away from becoming "almost, but not quite" once again.

## The Power of Purpose: Larry Merlo

Before Larry Merlo, CVS was primarily a retail pharmacy acquiring other retail pharmacies. It grew and grew, demonstrating agility and growth. However, it lacked a broader purpose beyond serving customer needs for prescriptions and consumer goods. Larry, a pharmacist by trade, transformed this drugstore company into a diversified health organization.

In announcing his retirement from the CEO role and resignation from the company board of directors, Larry wrote: "When I took on the role of CEO 10 years ago, my overarching objective was to transform CVS Health into a new kind of diversified health service company. We needed to migrate away from a successful but traditional pharmacy organization into an innovative enterprise that could integrate that successful pharmacy franchise into the broader and larger healthcare spectrum."[9]

"Today, with an expansive physical presence in communities across the nation, CVS Health has the unmatched ability to meet consumers where they are, and provide the care and services they need, be it in person or with the unique virtual delivery capabilities that extend the company's physical presence in real time," he continued. "That's what I'm most proud of:

today, CVS Health is more than a corner drugstore. It is a diversified health services company serving the needs of more than 100 million Americans each year."[10]

Larry's North Star was his commitment to patients, born of his background as a community pharmacist. He succeeded in bringing that sense of purpose into CVS, intentionally transforming it from a gigantic drugstore chain into a diversified healthcare company. The company's purpose clearly articulates this mission: "Bringing our heart to every moment of your health."[11]

## The Crucible of Innovation: Martin Glenn

Martin Glenn has an impressive track record of instilling innovation and vitality when organizations need reinvention. For Walkers Crisps, a subsidiary of PepsiCo UK, the trend of health consciousness that swept the UK in the early 2000s was a major challenge. The flavor of the chips, a highly popular selling point, was based on frying in palmolein, which is extracted from palm oil and extremely high in saturated fat.[12]

Walkers' focus groups and public opinion were moving against snacks and other foods perceived as unhealthy. For Martin, that was a challenge he relished: changing the ingredients of the crisps to improve their nutritional value while leaving the traditional taste unchanged. It was a challenge indeed because oils that were lower in saturated fat (such as olive oil) tasted terrible.[13] Martin searched high and low for an alternative, talking to scientists, suppliers, and even scoping out what his competitors were doing.

Finally, Cargill, Walkers' supplier of industrial fat, suggested a breed of sunflower seeds with oil that was low in saturated fat. Even better, this oil didn't need to be chemically hardened or hydrogenated to be used in the factories as palm oil had been.

When tested, the crisps retained their signature taste. However, this type of sunflower seed oil was not only scarce; it was also 30 to 40 percent more expensive than palm oil. Deciding to take a calculated risk on sunflower seed oil, Martin authorized an investment in planting acres of sunflower fields in Eastern Europe to ensure sufficient supplies.[14]

However, with Walkers' market share falling and public trust eroding, Martin had to make an innovative move to bolster his prime brand. Over time, Walkers mixed the palm oil with sunflower seed oil 50/50, then quietly increased the percentages of sunflower seed oil. By the time the company launched a marketing campaign touting the healthier crisps, the saturated fat was cut by 70 percent.[15] Martin's agility pivot paid off.

## The Potency of Vitality: Satya Nadella

When Satya Nadella took over as the CEO of Microsoft, the company was less than the sum of its parts. While it had power and heft in a number of markets, the company lacked the cohesion and collaboration necessary to catapult it to the Thriving stage. More than eight years after he was hired as CEO, it's clear that Satya was the missing catalyst. In fact, as he shares in his book, *Hit Refresh*, he "put the company's culture at the top of our agenda. I said that we needed to rediscover the soul of Microsoft, our reason for being."[16] That meant in part looking at all of Microsoft and finding new and inventive ways to connect and integrate parts of the organization to create leading-edge value.

Of the 10 largest acquisitions in company history, seven have been made under Satya's leadership. The common theme of the acquisitions was to either enter into or fortify a market that Microsoft needed to increase the scope of its partnerships. The most recent—and largest—was the $75 billion acquisition of Activision Blizzard, a gaming company. As reported by the *Wall Street Journal*: "An acquisition also would mark the latest and biggest move by Microsoft Chief Executive Officer Satya Nadella to reshape Microsoft through a series of deals that have helped make the world's second highest-valued company a powerhouse in business computing and a rising giant in videogames."[17]

Growing the company's gaming business meshed well with Microsoft's growing heft in cloud computing, as the gaming ecosystem shifted increasingly toward cloud-based gaming and the metaverse, a virtual universe in which individuals can work, game, play, and shop via digital avatars.[18] Microsoft gained popular titles including the *Call of Duty* and *World of Warcraft* franchises, which may have helped it fend off upstart rivals in the gaming space, including Amazon and Google, as well as longtime gaming competitors such as Sony.[19]

Moving forward, Microsoft can use these franchises to feed its popular Game Pass service, which Satya frames as "a Netflix for games."[20] If the company chooses to exclusively offer these games on the Xbox, that would be a major blow to Sony's PlayStation gaming platform, a move it has already made with other acquisitions such as *Starfield* and *Elder Scrolls 6*, games acquired from Bethesda Studios.[21]

"Gaming is the most dynamic and exciting category in entertainment across platforms today and will play a key role in the development of metaverse platforms," said Nadella. "We're investing deeply in world-class content, community and the cloud to usher in a new era of gaming that puts players and creators first and makes gaming safe, inclusive and accessible to all."[22]

In a conference call announcing the acquisition, Satya said, "For us, when we think about acquisitions, we always start with our mission: to empower every person and every organization on the planet to achieve more. Activision Blizzard is one of the premier game publishers worldwide, and their mission to connect and engage the world through epic entertainment is deeply aligned with our own. Therefore, our ambition is to bring the joy and community of gaming to everyone on the planet."[23]

Though the acquisition was still being reviewed by various country governments as of this writing, there is no doubt that Satya and Microsoft will continue seeking new and better growth opportunities in service of their mission.

## Liftoff: the Power of the Thriving Principles Together

As we move on in this journey, our next chapter takes us to the true power of these characteristics when they work together. You've seen in this chapter how much leaders and organizations can accomplish even with two of these principles. With all three working together on a leadership and organization-wide basis, the foundation is laid for companies that can truly thrive.

## From Insight to Action

**Reflect:** Consider your recent performance as a leader. Which of the three Thriving principles is your "front burner," and which is your "back burner"? What evidence do you have?

**Experiment:** Engage a few trusted colleagues in private conversation. Share the definitions for the three "almost but not quite" types—Explorer, Evangelist, Brainstormer—and ask them which most represents you at this moment. What did you learn?

**Choose:** How will you continue building your front burner as a signature strength and begin improving your back burner? What actions will you take? And what improved outcomes do you want to experience as a result?

## PART 3

# BRINGING THRIVING TO LIFE TODAY AND TOMORROW

# CHAPTER 6

## Liftoff

### *The Power of All Three at Work*

When Edwin Hubble was born in 1889 in Marshfield, Missouri, the Milky Way was the only known galaxy within what was perceived as a static universe.[1] The study of astronomy and cosmology was limited by the state of telescope technology and the prevailing ideas about space.

Edwin relished exploration and knowledge, leading him to earn undergraduate degrees in math and astronomy from the University of Chicago.[2] A five-sport athlete, he played on the university's championship basketball team in 1909 and passed up an opportunity to train for the world heavyweight boxing championship.[3]

After earning a law degree at Oxford University during his tenure as a Rhodes scholar and briefly practicing law, Edwin returned to the University of Chicago to earn a PhD in astronomy. He focused his research on nebulae, which, at the time, was a name for permanent, cloudy areas observed outside the solar system. Whether they were part of our galaxy, the Milky Way, or other galaxies beyond our own could not be determined.[4] Many astronomers believed they were merely clouds of dust and gas.[5]

Upon concluding his studies, he served in World War I before accepting a job at the Mt. Wilson Observatory in Los Angeles, which provided access to the 100-inch Hooker telescope, the largest available at that time.[6] At age 30, his career as an astronomer and cosmologist was beginning.

Four years into his research into nebulae, on October 6, 1923, Edwin turned his telescope to a nebula in the constellation Andromeda. "What he saw astonished him. That tiny, blurry blob turned out to be a swirling disc of a trillion stars, gas, and dust," according to *Chosen Magazine*. "Hubble quickly realized it could be an entire galaxy—which at that time, was a revolutionary idea. Up until that day, the Milky Way was the whole Universe."[7]

His research not only substantiated the existence of other galaxies but also led to the creation of what is now known as the Hubble classification system for organizing the millions of galaxies in the universe.[8] Upending the field of cosmology, he also determined that the universe was not, in fact, static. Instead, it was dynamic, with galaxies moving away from each other at a rapid rate.[9] This phenomenon, initially known as Hubble's law, is now known as the Hubble-Lemaître law, to honor Georges Lemaître, a Belgian Catholic priest, mathematician, astronomer, and professor of physics at the Catholic University of Louvain.[10] Lemaître described the expansion of the universe five years before Hubble did.[11]

"By 1929, Hubble had completely reimagined our place in the universe," noted NASA.[12] This discovery precipitated the concept of the "big bang"—the idea that the universe began with an explosion of unimaginable force.[13]

The European Space Agency put it this way: "It was a revelation and overturned the conventional view of a static Universe by showing that the Universe itself was expanding. More than a decade earlier, Einstein himself had bowed to the observational wisdom of the day and corrected his equations, which had originally predicted an expanding universe. Now Hubble demonstrated that Einstein had been right in the first place."[14]

Imagine living in a world with one fixed solar system and galaxy. Within that world, limitations are inherent. When Edwin blew up the notion of a fixed universe, he opened the door for uncertainty and creativity. No longer was there only one solar system and one galaxy that existed in a certain way. Instead, there were galaxies upon galaxies, planets upon planets. There was growth and expansion that scientists and individuals could barely comprehend. Edwin threw what was a fixed world into ambiguity.

"Equipped with his five senses, man explores the universe around him and calls the adventure Science," said Edwin.[15] To succeed in his career, he had to stay committed to his purpose of exploring the universe while remaining open to whatever the evidence in front of him showed. Clearly, Edwin's sense of curiosity supported his historic achievements.

Edwin also benefitted from the work of prior astronomers, including the largely forgotten Henrietta Swan Leavitt.[16] Henrietta pioneered a critical method for measuring distance through space, which gave Edwin the formula he needed to understand that the scope of the universe extended far beyond our own galaxy. As a woman in the early twentieth century, she wasn't allowed to touch a telescope; instead, she studied pictures obtained by telescopes to extend our knowledge of the universe.[17] If not for the gender bias rife in science in the early twentieth century, the Hubble Space Telescope might instead have been the Swan Leavitt Telescope.

Edwin and Henrietta opened our eyes to a whole new universe. Until then, we only saw what fit the beliefs of the time. For leaders, this raises an important question: What limitations am I putting on what I see? We all have the metaphorical equivalent of that early, limited view of the universe in what we think is possible.

Make no mistake: there is more beyond what we currently see.

To bring you fully into an understanding of Thriving, in this chapter we'll start by outlining the steps you can take to experiment with a Thriving state of mind. Then, we show you common entry points into Thriving, including new mindsets and actions. Finally, you'll learn how what we call "crucible experiences" offer the potential to create Thriving at an even higher level.

## The Power Triad

In Chapter 1, we introduced the three key principles that distinguish Thriving leaders. Now, it's time to demonstrate why these three, in dynamic balance, are necessary to create and sustain a high-performing culture. Leaders, teams, and organizations must put these principles into practice and continually finetune them to achieve outstanding outcomes. That's because each principle establishes a certain type of force:

- **Purpose:** Creates forward-looking momentum through collective striving for impact
- **Vitality:** Emphasizes continuity by creating a sense of energy, integration, and connection
- **Agility:** Adjusts to change by continually seeking growth and the most effective pathways

When a rocket takes off, our perception would have us believe that it travels in a straight line. In fact, that rocket is constantly tilting off course. A gyroscope inside the rocket helps to counterbalance the forces at play, with constant calibrations, some in mere nanoseconds, to maintain a successful flight path.

Just like the rocket and its three enabling forces, your leadership can't lift off and maintain course to achieve your goals without these three principles acting in concert. The Thriving state represents your internal gyroscope.

As we noted in Chapter 5, if you have elements of purpose and agility but not vitality, you won't have the power to stay on course for the journey. If you have agility and connection without purpose, you don't know where you're going. Finally, if you have purpose and connection without agility, there's no ability to adapt and change to shifting circumstances along the way.

## The Four-Step Cycle That Changes Everything—Literally

How do you internalize these principles so you can execute against them effectively and consistently? While there can be many ups and downs on the journey of growth, we've learned through decades of working with clients that this effort involves an integrated four-step cycle (Figure 6.1).

1. Awareness
2. Intention
3. Choice
4. Practice

**FIGURE 6.1** The Four-Step Cycle That Changes Everything

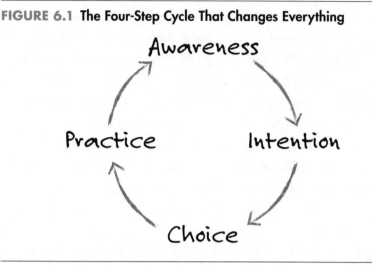

This isn't unique to Thriving. In fact, this approach is built into virtually all development and educational efforts. Whether you use a self-guided process like this book or work with a trainer, teacher, or coach who utilizes a similar system, some type of strategy based on human behavioral change is the key to ultimate success.

Let's put this into simple terms. If you imagine your own leadership capabilities for a moment, it's likely you have one or more areas you'd like to work on. Perhaps you received some feedback from a colleague or a boss and you've become *aware* it's time for an improvement.

From that sense of *awareness*, you typically set an *intention* about how you'd like to shift your thinking, behaviors, and results on that topic. "I would like to work on . . ." or maybe a more specific example: "I intend to delegate more work to my direct reports so they feel empowered and trusted." There can't be true awareness without honest soul-searching. In other words, you need to have the ability to honestly assess your shortcomings as well as the willingness to change whatever's not working.

From there, you can reflect further to understand the decisions you make currently that are not aligned with that intention. You can create an alternative list of approaches you'd like to try instead of your default behavior. Now you have created a *choice* for yourself. When you encounter such a conflict, what will you decide to do?

This is a key point on the cycle. It's relatively straightforward to decide how you theoretically might prefer to respond. But it's quite another to choose a different path in reality. We typically don't have much muscle memory or a well-worn path that supports this new approach, so it can feel a bit awkward at first. This is because your neural network hasn't yet established such a path, so the new behavior feels more difficult. That's why it's so important to *practice* the new choice in many different scenarios, so you become increasingly comfortable with it.

To summarize: a Thriving state is achievable when you focus your *awareness* on your current state, create new *intentions* that align with a Thriving state, define new *choices* you will make in support of it, and *practice, practice, practice*!

Recall the quote we mentioned earlier: "Becoming a leader is synonymous with becoming yourself. It is precisely that simple, and it is also that difficult."[18]

Consider the personal example of deciding to run a marathon. Perhaps you read about a well-known marathon, such as the Boston Marathon or New York City Marathon; or maybe you know someone who participated in those or other races. Something inspires you to imagine yourself accomplishing that feat. It enlivens you. That's where *awareness* begins.

At a certain point, you decide that you want to run a marathon. That's where *intention* begins. You look at your schedule and sign up for a marathon that fits in with your other activities. Your decision creates a domino effect as you determine how you need to change your routine to align with your desire to complete a marathon. Perhaps you find a training program or join a running club. You may also sign up for other, shorter races before the marathon so that you are fully ready.

Once you've set the intention of running a marathon, your *choices* will either reinforce your intention or undermine it. On a regular basis, you'll have the opportunity to train to move closer to reaching your goal, or to skip your training in favor of other activities such as sleeping late, surfing the internet, or going out with friends. To support your goal, you may need to improve your nutrition, cutting back on fast food and junk food and eating more protein, vegetables, and healthy foods. The more decisions you make that support your ultimate objective, the easier it will be to continue to move in that direction. However, if your intention isn't strong, you may undermine yourself by not sticking to your training schedule and/or eating poorly.

Finally, whether you will actually be able to complete the marathon depends on consistent *practice*, not just with generally healthy behaviors but also your training regimen. Many experienced runners recommend a training schedule that lasts between 16 and 20 weeks—four or five months.[19] During that period of time, you gradually increase the distance of your runs so that you build capacity to complete a 26.2-mile marathon. While recommendations vary depending on your level of fitness and the specific training program, most programs recommend at least one long run a week of 16 to 20 miles. These schedules usually include cross-training, incorporating rest days, and a variety of running activities such as interval training and sprints.

We can also examine this cycle through specific individual changes. When we think about the most effective leaders out there, such as Satya Nadella, we can go back in their lives and see where deep practice in an area of development helped propel them forward.

Satya shared in his book a vulnerable and candid story about how he became aware of his own empathy gap early in his career. A hiring manager at Microsoft asked him what appeared to be a random question. "Imagine you see a baby lying in the street and the baby is crying. What do you do?" he asked. Satya said without thinking that he would call 911. Upon hearing that, the manager walked him out of his office and told him, "You need some empathy, man. If a baby is lying on the street crying, pick up the baby."[20]

Through this new sense of *awareness*, Satya was forced to pay attention to the feedback and reflect on what it meant for him. This experience, combined with the birth of his son a few years later, caused him to create a new *intention* for himself, which prompted an exploration of what empathy means for him and how it can be fostered. He began to make new and different *choices* about the mindset he would bring to life and work, and the actions he would take. Over time he has *practiced* putting empathy front and center in his interactions and come to new conclusions, such as "life's experience has helped me build a growing sense of empathy for an ever-widening circle of people," and begun to deepen the connection between technology, the interactions among people, and how empathy is sustained.

Empathy is now widely considered to be one of Satya's super-powers that enable his leadership, and Microsoft, to seemingly defy the gravity of this chaotic world and lead through any-thing. It's important to note that it didn't start that way. Yet with this four-step cycle, and a clear idea of the critical few things to improve, all things are possible.

And it doesn't need to stop with one trait. Throughout his career, he would acquire new and better skills across many dimensions, essentially building the muscles he knew he needed for the future. Then, as he needed to grow in other areas, he began to add other principles. By the time he got to the CEO chair, he had developed capabilities that have changed the way his brain functions—literally!—and the way he interacts with others and performs on a daily basis.

## Breaking the Cycle Down

Here is how this cycle works in the context of Thriving.

### Awareness

To start, you must endeavor to become aware of your strengths and development areas when it comes to purpose, vitality, and agility. That's where your familiarity with the material in the first part of this book comes in. Take some time to consider how you stack up to the Thriving principles. Solicit input from the people you trust the most. Once you have a good idea of where you stand regarding the Thriving ideal, you'll know where you need to put in some work. The principles are not something that you internalize in five minutes. Instead, becoming a Thriving individual is literally the work of a career and a lifetime. When you understand that possibilities exist outside of your range of experience, you expand your awareness, which increases your options.

### Intention

Before you can change your behavior, you need to set a conscious intention to change. That intention helps you develop a better sense of what helps you achieve your goal and what doesn't serve you. The more important this goal is to you, the stronger your intentions will be. Change is difficult; that's why you must be convinced, in your heart, that this change is positive, necessary, and achievable. You also need support, which is why coaching can have such a powerful impact. Think of the best coach as a lead member of your personal board of directors—someone who knows you inside and out, who can act as a kind accountability partner, helping you get where you want to go.

## Choice

Once you're aware of your current behavior and how it compares to your ideal, you can take concrete steps to move toward your goal, harnessing attention and intention. Your awareness and intention create a desire to close the gap between who you are today and who you want to be in the future. That's where choice lives. Because you understand what you're doing and how it isn't leading to the ideal outcomes you'd like to achieve, you gain more of an ability to shape your own mind and behavior.

That leads to experimentation to learn what might bring you closer to where you want to be. You acquire the ability to do more of this, turn that up, turn that down, try again, make mistakes, be creative, be different. One caveat—don't expect 100 percent success right away. It's a good idea to set interim goals because if you try to do too much too quickly, you're setting yourself up for failure.

Just like with exercise, you build your muscle over time. Consistent choices to move your behavior in the right direction will add up. As you progress toward your goal, you can employ the power of imagination, encouraging yourself by envisioning what it will be like when you finally achieve your goal.

## Practice

By consistently building a new pattern of behavior based on awareness, intention, and choice, you will bring yourself closer to achieving your goal. Like training for a marathon, every day you need to be motivated to continue on your journey by engaging in the right behaviors and abandoning any that take you off track. Your coach and personal board of directors can help you evaluate your progress and create new interim goals to keep you moving toward the end goal. Inevitably, you'll backslide from time to time. This isn't the time to beat yourself up; instead, celebrate the progress you've made by recognizing that you now know what *not* to do. As Ed shares with clients, "Think in terms of degrees of improvement, not in absolutes." In other words, slow and steady really can win the race.

— — —

This four-step process is validated by neuroscience. Our brains develop in response to behavior. When you do something, the brain interprets either a positive or negative reaction. That results in the brain either reinforcing that behavior, and the synapses related to it, or disregarding it. That builds and changes your neural networks and creates a different you.

When, for instance, you decide to emphasize a Thriving principle such as agility by becoming a better listener, you start with an awareness that your listening skills could use some improvement. The next time you're in a meeting, you might stop playing with your phone or letting your mind drift off and choose to actively listen by asking questions and restating what you've heard, encouraging the speakers and helping them clarify their thinking. Over time, you maintain an intention to continue to be a better listener in different aspects of your life. You'll find ways to continue to practice at every opportunity. As with building muscle, leadership growth comes through deliberate practice and a lot of reps. Go for one more!

## Helpful Hacks—Doorways into the Thriving State

The Thriving State is a house with many doorways. In the course of our work, we've experienced leaders discovering many of these doorways—or practices—for themselves that help them create and sustain Thriving. In fact, we don't supply a comprehensive list or force certain practices onto leaders, because there are likely as many entry points as there are people. However, we have identified some of the consistently utilized practices that demonstrably lead to a Thriving state (Figure 6.2.)

---

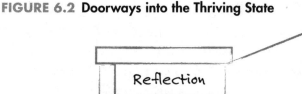

**FIGURE 6.2 Doorways into the Thriving State**

Reflection
Gratitude
Presence
Ambition
Failure
Acceptance
Listening
Crucibles

---

### Reflection

We mentioned the Reflective Thinker archetype in the agility principle, but this practice can and does apply to any Thriving principle. Reflective leaders consistently and thoughtfully create space between an event and their reaction to that event. Instead of immediately reacting, they take time to think the situation through, notice their own energy and emotions, solicit different opinions, and then respond. Outside of situations demanding an immediate response, reflective leaders carve white space into their calendars that ensures they can think, explore new ideas, learn, or just *be*. Phil Jackson is one of the best examples of a reflective leader we've seen. Of course, Phil was a believer in and a practitioner of overt methods of reflection, such as meditation. He encouraged his players to not only engage in meditation but also actively seek to adopt a more reflective state of mind. He describes some of his techniques in his book, *Eleven Rings*:

> *Another way I pushed the envelope was to have experts come in and teach the players yoga, tai chi, and other mind-body techniques. I also invited guest speakers—including a nutritionist, an undercover detective, and a prison warden—to show them new ways of thinking about difficult problems. Sometimes, when we were traveling short distances— between Houston and San Antonio, for instance—we'd load everybody onto a bus to give them a chance to see what the world looked like beyond the airport waiting rooms.*[21]

Leveraging reflection, through whatever techniques seem relevant, creates room for innovation and curiosity, and even learning from past experiences or failures. We mentioned earlier that Thriving leaders become the calm center in the midst of any storm. This is a critical practice that will get you there.

## Gratitude

Gratitude-centered leaders take nothing for granted; instead, they seek to view their world through a more balanced perspective by leveraging the lens of appreciation. For years, Dustin coached a veteran CEO who was generally optimistic and enthusiastic. At one point, however, Dustin noticed that this individual was flat, and his world was gray. Buckling under the weight of a divorce and some professional adversity, this leader had hit a bad spot.

Dustin advised him to start a gratitude journal, writing down the things he was grateful for in the morning and at night. "I'd like you to capture what you're grateful for—in life, in business, and whatever else you want to think about," he said. This CEO was skeptical, but he started working on it anyway. "He came back to me, re-energized, saying, 'My God, this works. It all looks different: the people that annoyed me look different, my business looks different, and my family looks different.'"

Gratitude creates fertile ground for improved clarity, leadership, and performance. Thriving leaders are not superhuman, but they are highly aware of what it feels like for their perspective to skew their mood or state of mind. In many of those cases, Thriving leaders find they are overly focused on things that are not working well in the moment, rather than appreciating the broader spectrum of things in their life—which includes a huge number that actually are working! For the vast majority of us in the developed world, our lives are probably 80 to 90 percent satisfactory. Yet we often allow bad situations, which are usually temporary, to dominate our thinking. Gratitude and appreciation are tools that help us bring things back into balance, which improves our state of mind and our ability to perform at any given moment.

## Presence

Thriving leaders live in the present moment because there is nothing else—anything else is a distraction. As the saying goes, yesterday is history, tomorrow is a mystery, and today is a gift.

For Michael Jordan, the present moment was a key to his success. "Why would I think about missing a shot I haven't taken?" he asked rhetorically in *The Last Dance*, a documentary about his basketball career.[22] For Michael, paying attention to a shot that wasn't in the here and now took his attention away from the present moment. His biographer put it this way: "[Michael's] gift was not that he could jump high, run fast, or shoot a basketball. His gift was that he was completely present. And that was the separator."[23]

Moving away from the present into the future or the past paves the way for distraction and failure. Focus instead on what the moment demands of you and how you can apply your capacities to create success. While this may seem overly "Zen" or even counterintuitive, Thriving leaders understand the importance, as Ed refers to it, of "strategically applying their presence." The leaders we've coached work hard to improve their ability to be present, which is often noticed quickly by others. When people leave an interaction with them, they feel special and important, like the leader truly heard them. This is not only great for the employee, but healthy for the leader. As you can imagine, this feeling has become much rarer in our dramatically distracted and multitasking world.

## Ambition

Thriving leaders are ambitious for impact. Personal, self-serving ambition isn't meaningful to them. Instead, they want to create a better world—or fulfill a larger purpose—through the platform of their work. They want to create good that lasts beyond themselves. Think of the often-referenced quote from Steve Jobs, who, while recruiting John Sculley to be the CEO of Apple, asked him, "Do you want to sell sugar water for the rest of your life or come with me and change the world?"[24] Thriving leaders typically view their work as part of a larger mission or noble cause. That energy often influences others and becomes a talent and customer magnet.

It is invaluable to take time to make connections between your company and product or service to a larger purpose beyond making money and creating shareholder value. What would be the full impact of your ambition? What type of a world are you focused on creating? Larry Merlo, former CEO of CVS, is a great example of this kind of leader. He never forgot his roots, which helped create the ambition that ultimately led him to lead and shape a company dedicated to transforming community health. As was written during his tenure, "Under Merlo's leadership, CVS Health is pioneering a bold new approach to total health by making quality healthcare more affordable, accessible, simple, and seamless. CVS Health is community based and locally focused, engaging consumers with the care they need when and where they need it."[25]

When ambition for the business, team, and impact outweighs personal ambition to such a degree, it means that Thriving leaders can create and maintain a drive for bigger, more impactful goals. At that point, it is not about them. It's about the impact of the cause.

## Failure

One of our favorite Winston Churchill quotes captures this element. He stated: "Success is not final; failure is not fatal: it is the courage to continue that counts."[26] In our modern culture, as often as you hear leaders paying lip service to wanting to "fail fast," the truth is that failures are often not well tolerated, let alone learned from. Many leaders spend a lot of time avoiding risk (or taking a wise risk!) in order to avoid failure at nearly any cost.

So it's even more meaningful in this context that Thriving leaders learn from, rather than run away from, failure. They treat failure as a learning experience rather than a dead end in and of itself. Consider again Apple founder Steve Jobs. Nine years after he founded Apple, the board removed him from any responsibilities, so he quit.[27] After a few months, he founded NeXT, a new computer company, and acquired the small studio that would become Pixar Animation Studios.[28] Eleven years later, in 1996, Apple acquired NeXT; in 1997, Steve resumed his role as Apple CEO.

Reflecting on the experience of leaving Apple, Steve later said, "I didn't see it then, but it turned out that getting fired from Apple was the best thing that could have ever happened to me. The heaviness of being successful was replaced by the lightness of being a beginner again, less sure about everything. It freed me to enter one of the most creative periods of my life."[29] Thriving leaders view failure as information that helps them make better choices and decisions in the future. As Robert Allen said, "There is no failure. Only feedback."[30]

## Acceptance

All too often, when reality conflicts with our views, we construct our own alternative universe. That universe aligns with our internal reality but leaves us disconnected from the truth and much more likely to take ineffective actions. Thriving leaders resist that impulse, because ultimately, it is impossible to impose our worldview on reality. Yet all things are possible if we acknowledge reality and build a plan based on it. The Stockdale Paradox, outlined in Jim Collins's book *Good to Great*, states that positive change begins when we can confront brutal facts while believing that we will ultimately prevail.[31]

Brian Chesky, CEO of Airbnb, is a master of acceptance. Early in the Covid-19 pandemic, few executives wanted to accept the harsh realities of Covid. Dustin and Ed heard from many leaders who were taking a "wait and see" approach. But Brian trusted the projections in his leading indicator data, and realized that Covid presented an unprecedented threat. Acceptance of those hard facts enabled him and his entire organization to get out in front of the disruption so that they could make and implement the necessary difficult choices that would preserve Airbnb's business fundamentals and organizational flexibility. You may remember what ultimately resulted from Brian's position of acceptance—Airbnb went public with one of the largest IPOs of 2020.[32]

## Listening

Thriving leaders regard listening as a foundational capability. They realize that it is impossible to uphold purpose, remain agile, and stay connected without superb listening skills. For a leader like Martin Glenn, who succeeded as the CEO of several organizations that were quite different from each other, listening was a key to his success. Coming from leading consumer brands such as Walkers, Pepsi, Birds Eye, and United Biscuits, Martin brought a focus on relationships, powered by listening, into his leadership of the UK Football Association. In introducing Glenn at the beginning of his tenure, the FA stated: "Putting fans first and building better relationships with the Premier League and the Football League are top of Martin Glenn's to-do list at the Football Association."[33]

On his first day at the helm of the Football Association, Martin said, "I am a big believer in relationships—not for the sake of them—but that relationships with honesty around objectives can always get things done. . . . You will get more deep-rooted improvement if you work together to drive to a common agenda, which is making the England teams more successful and improving grassroots football."[34] Relationships, especially those that achieve great things, start with being willing to listen for understanding. Change, on many levels, happens when we listen deeply. Deep listening is a muscle that must be continually exercised to flourish.

We've noticed that the best listeners actually listen to be persuaded. Most of us "listen to reply"—if, in fact, we are even paying attention. We listen to persuade others, rather than to be persuaded. But the Thriving leader often actively solicits and explores opinions in conflict with their own. They seek out contrary opinions because they understand that they must remain vigilant to avoid becoming overconfident and static in their approach. In the words of an article by Jack Zenger and Joseph Folkman in *Harvard Business Review*, good listeners are like trampolines. "They are someone you can bounce ideas off of— and rather than absorbing your ideas and energy, they amplify, energize and clarify your thinking. They make you feel better not merely by passively absorbing, but by actively suggesting. This lets you gain energy and height, just like someone jumping on a trampoline."[35]

Unfortunately, it's all too easy for veteran leaders to let their listening muscles atrophy, as the highly self-aware Disney CEO Bob Iger noted regarding his decision to initially retire in 2020: "Over time, I started listening less and maybe with a little less tolerance of other people's opinions. Maybe because of getting a little bit more overconfident in my own, which is sometimes what happens when you get built up. I became a little bit more dismissive of other people's opinions than I should have been. That was an early sign that it was time."[36] When he returned as CEO in 2022, one of his first steps was to conduct listening tours with both employees and customers before deciding on the changes he would implement.

## Crucibles: Necessary for Thriving

A crucible is a challenging, uncomfortable, maybe even painful experience—it could be an event, situation, or relationship—that will shape you in a transformational way. Crucibles can be life-changing events—such as divorce, job loss, or a major illness—or seemingly smaller events that provoke a similar response. A crucible offers the opportunity for change. Essentially, you can either run toward a crucible or run away from it. The crucible itself isn't as significant as what you become as a result of it.

We all have our crucibles. One question we sometimes ask in our executive coaching engagements is: "What are you running away from in this situation?" A crucible is usually something that you're avoiding or trying to control. In that state, you remain stuck. But when you embrace the crucible, you create the space for internal change and growth. Many crucibles are painful, difficult, or uncomfortable, which is why there's a tendency to try to avoid, control, or run away from them.

You're formed in a Thriving way only when you embrace the crucible and whatever lesson it's teaching you. Dustin's mentor John Clayton used to say that there's really no world champion in the 90-meter sprint—instead, the athlete who triumphs is the one who perseveres in the final 10 meters. While there may be many world-class sprinters out there who can cover 90 meters, only the very best can cross the finish line first.

Ed relates to this concept through the medium of personal fitness. In a quest to achieve a higher state of personal conditioning, Ed decided to improve his fitness. Among the techniques he's employing are those espoused by Tim Ferriss in his book *The 4-Hour Body*.[37] A key teaching is that to develop muscle strength through weight training, the last rep of the last set is what ultimately matters most. Where most people would stop is where those in search of a higher level of fitness must go. It's a place where you literally believe that you have nothing left to give, but if growth is the goal, you complete that last rep of the final set, or fail trying. The strength you gain builds during recovery after that final push. Ed's found that in fitness, like in leadership, growth comes from becoming one with the toughest moments and embracing them.

When you encounter a crucible, you experience it from a place of love or fear. Crucibles activate either the seeking system, which is our ventral striatum in the frontal lobe of the brain, or the fear system in the amygdala. The seeking system's natural tendencies are growth, resilience, innovation, collaboration, and possibility. The fear system's natural tendencies are controlling, fixing, focusing on self, and avoidance.

What event or experience serves as your crucible is less important than your response to that crucible. Thriving leaders embrace crucibles, while non-Thriving leaders avoid them. Jerry Rice, the American football player, put it this way: "Today I will do what others won't, so tomorrow I can do what others can't."[38]

Tom Brady, the seven-time Super Bowl–winning quarterback who retired in early 2023, is famous for overcoming adversity and turning crucibles into victory. "Both personally and professionally, I have faced challenges and sought out people who had better professional insights where I could use their experiences to learn from," he said. "In my young career I doubted myself a lot. When I saw things that weren't going my way, I thought I was the victim of circumstance. But when I changed, shifted my view and my mind to say 'I am not a victim, why don't I empower myself' I could grow in ways I was struggling. Through working with psychologists and others, I learned you have to face challenges and look at them as opportunities for growth."[39]

In high school and college, Brady wasn't necessarily the best player on his teams, or even the best quarterback. Throughout his college career at the University of Michigan, he was competing for the starting quarterback role. In the NFL, he was the 199th pick in the 2000 draft and not expected to stand out or even necessarily succeed in the NFL. "I was never the fastest; I was never the biggest or strongest. I had to compete as hard as I could. That taught me how to work harder. And here's what I figured out: if things weren't really working out for me, in high school, in college, early in my pro career, my solution was always to work harder and internalize. That way, whenever I got an opportunity, I was always prepared."[40]

Another example of a Thriving leader who led by embracing challenge rather than running from it is Umran Beba, former senior vice president and chief global diversity and engagement officer for PepsiCo. Umran took over as acting head for Pepsi-Co's Asia, Middle East, and Africa (AMEA) region after her dear friend and boss Saad Abdul Latif suddenly died in August 2013.[41] Pivoting from her role as SVP and chief human resources officer of Pepsi AMEA, Umran succeeded in continuing Saad's initiatives while exceeding sales and profitability targets. Engagement scores for executives, managers, and employees were among the highest in all of PepsiCo history. Umran has always been willing to step into the crucible, learn, and help others achieve great things.

Then there's Ray Dalio, Founder and CIO Mentor at Bridge-water Associates, LP, one of the most successful hedge funds in the world. Ray formulated a helpful equation: Pain + Reflection = Progress. He describes it this way in a LinkedIn post: "There is no avoiding pain, especially if you're going after ambitious goals. Believe it or not, you are lucky to feel that kind of pain if you approach it correctly, because it is a signal that you need to find solutions so you can progress. If you can develop a reflexive reaction to psychic pain that causes you to reflect on it rather than avoid it, it will lead to your rapid learning/evolving."[42]

After the sudden death of his 42-year-old son, Devon, on December 17, 2020, Ray put these principles to a real test.[43] "Because my son's life was more important than my own life and everything I have, when we learned of his death on December 17, it was like a bomb went off that tore my wife and I and our family up. At the time, it was difficult to process emotionally and intellectually, yet I had to decide what to do to deal with these traumas. Meditation helped calm things down and provided me and my other family members who meditate greater equanimity and clarity."[44]

Ray goes on to describe how he and his family retreated to a quiet place and spent time together after the funeral, which gave them freedom to think, feel, and grieve in their own ways. Placing this loss in a larger context was also helpful. "It didn't take long for me to realize that the devasting experience my family and I were going through was being experienced by many people at the same time (because of Covid and because of other reasons), which both made me feel for them and help me deal with my loss better."

The experiences of Tom Brady, Umran Beba, Ray Dalio, and countless others demonstrate that when we face challenges and choices in our lives with awareness, intention, choice, and practice, we grow and change in amazing ways. We can lead out of fear or we can lead out of love. We always try to remember that we will never be able to understand someone else's internal experience, even if we've been through a life event that seems exactly the same. Each of us is unique and experiences life in a unique way. Our job as human beings is to do whatever we can to bridge the gaps that seem to stand between us, to create as much of a common understanding as possible.

Years ago, Ed interviewed dozens of executives for a leadership study on global organizations. One of the leaders, who had been a successful head of various institutions, said that the reality of leadership meant being the individual who was asked to endure "the pain of standing in the gap between what the organization is today and what the organization aspires to become in the future." This, we believe, is the essential crucible for leaders and organizations who seek to thrive while defying gravity. In the largest sense, life itself is the ultimate crucible. None of us knows what's around the next corner. All we can do is control how we respond to it—with love, or with fear.

Now that you've learned about the components of Thriving and how to establish a Thriving mindset, next we drill down even further into the Thriving leaders of the future, distilling the characteristics that ensure you can lead through anything that comes your way in an exceptionally disrupted reality.

## From Insight to Action

**Reflect:** What is one development area where you would like to apply the Four-Step Cycle of awareness, intention, choice, and practice?

**Experiment:** Engage a close colleague or trusted friend. Share your development goal and explain the cycle to them. Ask for feedback to clarify your goal and the specific shift you'd like to make. What did you learn?

**Choose:** What is the goal you are committing to? What is your timeline to achieve it? How will you know you're on the right track?

# CHAPTER 7

# You

## The Thriving Leader of the Future

As part of the process for a consulting engagement that shall remain anonymous, Dustin interviewed an organization's entire executive team.

In every conversation, each member from the executive team asked: "Have you spoken to the senior VP yet?" Let's call that senior VP Joe.

Each time, Dustin replied in the negative, because, as it happened, Joe was one of the last on his list.

Finally, the day arrived when Dustin met with Joe for his interview.

"Dustin, I know you're probably a nice guy and what you do is really good, but it won't work here," Joe said.

"Okay," Dustin replied. "That takes some pressure off. I'm interested in learning why you think this won't work."

"Look," Joe said. "We've had all the other big consulting firms, we've all been involved, they've done their stuff, and it hasn't changed a thing."

"So I'll show up," Joe continued. "I'll be at the kickoff event, I'll participate, but just don't get too excited."

Dustin nodded.

After a moment's reflection, Dustin said, "Just let me check again to make sure I understand what's going on."

Joe nodded agreeably.

"They were all different consulting firms," Dustin said.

"Yes," Joe replied.

"Different approaches?" Dustin asked.

"Yep," Joe confirmed.

"Different methodologies?" Dustin inquired.

"Sure," he said.

"Yeah, we've tried everything," Joe continued, shaking his head, and looking a bit sorrowful.

Dustin sat for a minute, thinking, then he spoke: "So the only constant is you."

Joe looked perplexed.

"You might want to think about that," Dustin said.

Two days later, Dustin and his consulting team were at a dinner with the senior executives, after the first day of their leadership off-site. Dustin was talking privately to the CEO when Joe came up and asked if he could have a few minutes with both of them.

Dustin looked at the CEO, and he nodded.

"Dustin," said Joe. "I want to be the culture champion for this whole organization."

The CEO laughed.

"I mean it," said Joe seriously.

"I'm getting married next week for the second time," he confessed.

"I realized after we talked that my first wife was right about what she said about me," Joe continued. "I was doing at home the same things I was doing at work, and it drove her nuts. I think you just saved my second marriage."

Joe's story is a great example of the power of awareness and the intention to make new and better choices. It came not a moment too soon for that team.

What we have learned through the years is that until individual leaders take responsibility for themselves and their impact on an organization, attempts at cultural change are doomed to fail. That's because organizations ultimately become shadows of their leaders, a concept that we'll discuss in depth in this chapter.

One leader we worked with, Phil Swash, put it this way: "I finally realized that anyone can copy our tech and our process, but they cannot copy our culture. And I realized that it starts with me and my team." Phil went on to become CEO of GKN Automotive, a leading automotive drive systems manufacturer based in the United Kingdom.

The most successful leaders we work with understand that, fundamentally, Thriving begins with them.

This chapter is about you.

We want to offer a different angle to explore this idea. Let's begin with the extreme *antithesis* of Thriving via the story of Elizabeth Holmes and Theranos. While it's highly unlikely that you're doing what Elizabeth did, within this story are the seeds of issues that we all face.

At one time or another, you—and we, and everyone else out there—will confront an issue that tests your willingness to be honest with yourself, to learn, adjust, adapt, and change. Ultimately, Thriving—or choosing not to thrive—is about taking responsibility. Elizabeth's story illustrates what can happen when there's an extreme abdication of responsibility. The impact, as you may know, was catastrophic not only for her and her organization, but also for many others. As we write this, she's been sentenced to 11 years in prison after being convicted of wire fraud and conspiracy.[1]

## Anti-Thriving: A Case Study

Silicon Valley promises to leverage technology to revolutionize time-consuming and expensive processes. But in some cases, when it comes to ensuring that these promises are realized, all bets are off. The results of these failures often appear in dysfunctional corporate cultures long before cracks materialize in products, services, and financial results.

That was the case with Theranos, the infamous health-tech startup that vowed to deliver robust lab results from just a few drops of blood.[2] The company's executives were never able to get the technology behind this idea to work, yet the company bamboozled businesses, individuals, and the world into believing that they did. Years before the widespread fraud that characterized the company's operations and finances was revealed, secrecy, paranoia, and control ruled the organization's corporate culture.[3] Despite the toxic culture, unknown by many in the outside world, Theranos was a darling of both Silicon Valley and Wall Street.

Founded in 2003 by 19-year-old Stanford dropout Elizabeth Holmes, Theranos was a magnet for venture capital and media attention. But a closer look at the company revealed a slew of troubling issues, many stemming from the organization's struggle to deliver on its primary mission: producing lab tests that could accurately diagnose medical conditions.[4]

To perpetuate the Theranos myth, Elizabeth employed nondisclosure agreements and organizational silos while exploiting internal governance failures and a lack of regulatory supervision to ensure that any dirty laundry remained private, far below the public radar.[5]

Reporter John Carryrou, who broke the Theranos scandal while at the *Wall Street Journal*, went on to publish a bestselling book, *Bad Blood: Secrets and Lies in a Silicon Valley Startup*, about the company.[6] According to an article published by the MIT Sloan School of Management, John believed that "the company's culture of extreme secrecy and swift retaliation against anyone who went against the grain set the stage for its eventual failure. 'There was sort of an Omertà [a code of silence as practiced by the Mafia] in that from the early stages of the company—and it got worse and worse—there was really unethical behavior and employees who would try to raise questions were either fired, marginalized, or left of their own volition,'" he told an audience in an October 2018 presentation at the MIT Sloan School of Management.[7]

As the company unraveled, Elizabeth continued to fly across the country in her private jet, accompanied by a personal security detail. Her legal bills, totaling millions, were covered by the company, as was a $25,000 monthly retainer for her personal publicist.[8] The corporate drama finally ended when the SEC forced Elizabeth to give up her voting control of the company as well as a substantial portion of her equity stake in March 2018.[9]

In January 2022, a jury convicted Elizabeth of one count of conspiracy and three counts of wire fraud in connection with the multimillion-dollar corporate failure.[10] Besides the implosion of the company, the lives of tens of thousands of individuals who received inaccurate lab results, some for cancer and HIV, were negatively impacted.[11] Theranos's deeply flawed corporate culture perpetuated multiple bad actions and crimes.

As we've described in the first six chapters of this book, Thriving leaders embody three key characteristics: purpose, vitality, and agility. To briefly recap, purpose embodies a sense of direction and clarity; vitality typifies energy, presence, and connection; and agility represents creativity and innovation. When we stated early on in this chapter that Elizabeth could be described as an anti-Thriving leader, we weren't joking.

While there's no doubt that Elizabeth initially had a noble purpose in founding Theranos, she ultimately used that avowed mission to manipulate employees to continue to work on failing technologies.[12] In their hearts, purposeful leaders demonstrate alignment between their personal and professional personas and values. There's no room in that description for exploiting others for a leader's own gain.

Although agile leaders like Elizabeth inspire others, they don't use their search for knowledge and growth to prop up a clearly failing enterprise with lies, fraud, and manipulation. Instead of motivating others to learn and improve, she used fear and control to isolate her employees from one another, creating silos to prevent her misdeeds from being discovered.

Undoubtedly, Elizabeth had to expend a phenomenal amount of energy to keep Theranos afloat and her teams focused on their work. But this isn't the kind of energy a true Thriving leader applies. Instead of generating trust and vitality, Elizabeth fostered mistrust, suspicion, and anxiety.

The story of Theranos is fascinating precisely because the leadership failures were so egregious. We'll never know how Elizabeth morphed from an enthusiastic entrepreneur who wanted to save the world into a convicted felon. What we do know is that each of us is presented with smaller decisions on a day-to-day basis, decisions where any of us can all too easily cross invisible lines away from—instead of toward—Thriving.

We aren't talking about perfection. No one is, or will ever be, perfect. We're talking about the fine line between direction and dictatorship, between vitality and mania, and between agility and fabrication.

Because Thriving is based on self-knowledge and self-awareness, we all bear the responsibility to develop and maintain an ethical compass that will ensure we stay honest with ourselves, our families, our friends, our teams, our organizations, our customers, our shareholders, and so on. Without honesty and accountability, there is no Thriving. The process of examining our motives, holding ourselves to the highest ethical standards, and striving to become better people never ends. If it does, beware. This, ultimately, is the lesson of Theranos. We've captured the essence of this dynamic relative to our Thriving model in Figure 7.1.

**FIGURE 7.1 The Anti-Thriving Leader**

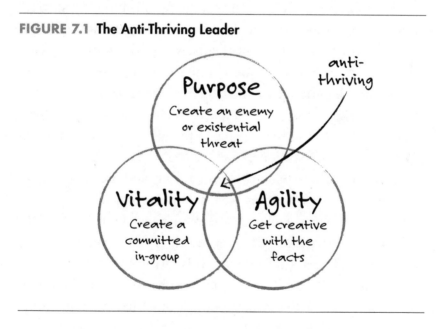

## Leadership Shadows

Without the correct mindset, no one and nothing—neither you, your team, nor your organization—can fully reach their potential. As disruption grows, whether from a pandemic, technological upheaval, a war, or inflation, Thriving is a critical prerequisite for success in a chaotic world. We've focused on leadership because where the leader goes, the organization follows. That's because, as we've underscored several times, organizations always become "shadows of their leaders." Larry Senn, who along with Jim Delaney founded culture-shaping firm Senn Delaney, coined this term more than 45 years ago.

What exactly does it mean that an organization is a shadow of its leaders? When new employees join an organization, there's a period in which they orient themselves to the company's culture. That doesn't just involve reading the employee handbook or getting a handle on the benefits. In addition to those critical pieces, they instinctively look to their coworkers and their leaders to understand how people in this new environment work together to get things done.

This is not about what the company's grandiose language on its website says or what they were told during their onboarding. Instead, they pay the closest attention to attitudes, behaviors, decisions, and responses. They gather clues from what they hear, what they read, and what they see. This is truly where the cultural rubber hits the road. If a company has a collaborative culture, like Microsoft, that's evident. If, on the other hand, an organization encourages secrecy, politics, and infighting, that is also clear.

"I observed that companies, like people, had personalities, and while some were healthy, most were like dysfunctional families," Larry said. "They had trust issues, turf issues, and resistance to change. The difference between working with

Sam Walton on the supply chain at Walmart and working with Woolworths was like night and day. It was clear one company would succeed and the other would fail because of the mindset and habits of the firms."[14]

His views on Woolworths and Walmart were accurate: Woolworths closed its last American stores in 1997, while Walmart has extended its domination of American retail.[15] In his meetings with the Walmart executive team, Larry could feel the energy and drive, while the atmosphere at Woolworths was like a morgue.

Just as children tend to imitate their parents, employees— though not children—tend to emulate their leaders. That means that as a leader, you need to understand that your employees will put your words and actions under a microscope. They will always be looking for the underlying reality or trying to interpret your unspoken messages. Why? Because their paycheck depends on it. Employees instinctually need to fit in. Whether or not you realize how influential your modus operandi is, your team or organization will seek to echo you. If, for example, you instinctively flinch at honest feedback, you'll quit getting it. In the same way, if you are truly open to it, you're more likely to actually receive it. There's no way to fake it. Just as your family knows you, your team and your organization know you, for good or ill.

When you step into a new organization, one of the first questions you ask yourself, whether you're aware of it or not, is "What's going on above me?" Once that's understood, most people tend to copy that behavior, sometimes even subconsciously. Whatever happens at the top of an organization ends up washing downhill to the bottom of the system. That's why when we lead corporate culture engagements, we sometimes experience the pushback we described in the opening of this chapter.

Teams want to know whether leadership is truly serious about change or not. If the change leaders say they want is not being role-modeled by that top leadership, the change will remain no more than lip service. And let us assure you—people are used to getting a lot of lip service!

As external disruption escalates, the very nature of business as usual has changed. In this environment, culture and leadership will ultimately make the difference between good and great. Too many leaders have made the mistake of believing that their differentiators involved only their products, services, processes, and structure. Those things, while critical, are typically sustained only through the short term. They can be, and often are, quickly copied by competitors.

The most difficult thing for a competitor to replicate is a healthy, high-performing culture that attracts and keeps the best talent and creates and sustains true innovation. This is the era of leadership—a time in which culture must come first. Not just because it's better for people: it's better for business, too.

## "Culture Accelerator" Leaders and Organizations Get Better Results

Our term for those who understand this dynamic is "Culture Accelerators." Leaders such as Satya Nadella, Sipho Maseko, Dominique Leroy, Brian Chesky, and Wendy Clark, former CEO of Dentsu, are all in our view, culture-first leaders. They understand that culture is the essential foundation for their company's success.

Wendy, who was hired as media and advertising giant Dentsu's CEO six months into the Covid-19 pandemic, immediately established a leadership style that combined transparency and clear vision. The pandemic turned the media and advertising industries upside down, which meant that Wendy had to not only demonstrate her vision but also execute it at the same time. "The people who dwell on the doing lose the plot and to what mountain they are climbing and the people too busy staring at the mountain don't ever get up there," she said. "You've got to have that real intersection of being able to think and do."[16]

To succeed in this journey, Wendy embraced and evangelized a concept she calls "radical collaboration." "The soft skills of emotional intelligence and human interactions are going to be absolutely crucial," she noted. "Baseline collaboration is not enough anymore, it's about radical collaboration, having a mindset for speed and agility, and being able to adapt to constantly shifting variables."[17]

Moving forward, Wendy focused the organization's vision in six areas: people, clients, work, financial, social impact, and company transformation. Each of these areas had specific goals, priorities, and metrics. During her first six months with the company, she reorganized around three service lines—creative, media, and customer experience management—while consolidating to six agency brands from more than 20. "We must make ourselves easier and more agile to do business with," Wendy said of the internal changes.[18]

In seeking to transform Dentsu's corporate culture, Wendy wanted to foster a sense of curiosity within the organization. "The mentality I would love our team to have is: listen, hear what clients are saying, talk about the challenges and then make suggestions around ways we can be helpful—if it's things we're not working on," she said. "I want us to have a constant, perpetual motion of 'What else can we do? How else can we be helpful? What resource [do you need]?'"[19] What Wendy is referencing is the essence of an accountable, customer-centric culture, which is a standout trait among high-performing organizations.

Leaders like Wendy who place culture front and center are more likely to demonstrate strong performance than those who don't. As mentioned earlier in this book, in 2021 a Heidrick & Struggles CEO survey revealed that companies that deliberately link culture and strategy while focusing on people first earn financial performance, assessed by three-year revenue compound annual growth rate (CAGR), more than double that of others in the survey—9.1 percent versus 4.4 percent. These results are consistent regardless of geography, sector, and size.[20]

Culture Accelerators are leaders who consistently and proactively nurture their organizational cultures. Thriving leaders and cultures demonstrate high levels of agility, collaboration, trust, coaching and feedback, and customer-facing accountability. For Wendy at Dentsu, this didn't mean putting operational success on the back burner—instead, it meant defining and supporting cultural transformation that would enable all other elements of the business to thrive.

Leaders from this category of accelerators who flourish at the peak of culture are known as "culture connectors." This is a distinct subset of leaders and companies who take their cultural strength to a whole new level. How exactly do they do this? By relentlessly focusing on clear, effective internal and external communication. Engagement is their byword.

To make this come alive in your organization, it has to be a passion—not lip service. Culture connectors share a personal commitment to focusing on culture by leading and living the culture they espouse. They find two-way dialogues with employees about the importance of culture, and its alignment with their business direction, particularly effective on an ongoing, consistent basis.

To win at culture going forward, you must commit and stay committed.

## How to Nurture Thriving

To thrive in this era of continual disruption, you must completely take responsibility for your personal leadership shadow and your organization's culture.

When discussing culture with leaders around the world, we often compare a company's culture with the operating system of a computer or smartphone. The operating system directs the devices to work in a certain way. Organizational culture is no different.

If a company's operating system is indeed its culture and an organization ultimately becomes the shadow of its leaders, that means you, the leader, are the source code. In other words, if you don't like your company culture, don't look at the people around you—look at yourself. They're doing what they are doing because you're doing what you're doing. And whatever it is that you're doing is what sets the trend.

Fortunately, you don't have to go at this backward. Ideally, you get your own intentions straight before you take on the big role, so that you're completely clear about who you are and what you stand for, as well as able to communicate those values and standards to your organization. If you can do that, you'll be like the leaders whose stories we've told in this book, where there is a healthy and effective cultural alignment.

Consider Bob Iger, who has served as CEO of the Walt Disney Company for more than 15 years, transforming Disney into a vertically integrated media company that includes Marvel Studios, Pixar, Lucasfilm, and 21st Century Fox.[21] Disney's stock gained 12.3 percent on an annualized basis during Bob's initial tenure, which ended in 2020 before continuing in 2022, significantly exceeding the gain of the S&P 500 of 6.8 percent annually during the same period.[22]

Bob excels at a combination of vision, communication, and execution similar to other Thriving leaders. "He worked to boost morale within the company by dismantling a management system that often pitted executives against one another," according to the *Los Angeles Times*. "He gave more autonomy to division heads who had chafed under relentless meddling by Disney's powerful strategic planning department."[23]

Bob believed that the marriage of Disney's franchise film strategy with its theme parks would maximize the value of the intellectual property they amassed during their acquisitions of film studios. The result included fresh attractions at Disney's Anaheim and Orlando theme parks based on Pixar and Star Wars. Instead of relying on third parties to fuel Disney, Iger created an end-to-end entertainment machine that had the chops to launch Disney+ and muscle into America's living rooms.[24]

Each of his acquisitions of franchise film studios, including Pixar, Marvel, Lucasfilm, and 20th Century Fox, built on Bob's commitment to nurturing relationships. In fact, one of Bob's first calls after he got the CEO position was to Steve Jobs. Steve had previously announced that due to discord with Disney's prior management he intended to sever ties with the company. "I had to repair the relationship," Bob recalled. "So, the day the board called me to say I was CEO . . . I decided to call my parents, my grown children, a couple of friends and Steve."[25]

Not only was Bob able to repair Disney's relationship with Pixar, but he also approached Jobs about what he termed "a crazy idea."[26] Believing that Disney's in-house studio was faltering in terms of creativity, Bob decided that the best way to restore the company's reputation for innovation was to buy Pixar.[27]

Iger told Bloomberg in an interview: "Anyone that knew Steve would know that, if you said to Steve, 'I have a crazy idea,' he would have to hear it right away." That turned out to be the case— and, according to Iger, Jobs responded, "Well, it's not that crazy."[28]

Soon after Iger proposed a potential acquisition of Pixar, they met and Jobs gave him a tour. Afterward, Iger recalls, "What I saw that day left me breathless—the level of talent and creative ambition, the commitment to quality, the story-telling ingenuity, the technology, the leadership structure, and the air of enthusiastic collaboration—even the building, the architecture itself," he wrote in his autobiography. "It was a culture that anyone in a creative business, in any business, would aspire to."[29]

With both Steve and Bob committed to the Pixar acquisition, the deal went through, resulting in a $7.4 billion valuation for Pixar. As a result, Steve became the largest Disney shareholder and received a seat on the board.[30]

As CEO at Disney, Bob sets clear priorities and emphasizes them repeatedly through communications to his teams and organization. "If you don't articulate your priorities clearly, then the people around you don't know what their own should be," he said. "Time and energy get wasted." He attributes his constant innovation to his "deep and abiding" sense of curiosity.[31]

Bob learned early on to distill his ideas down into three key priorities, which he used to drive Disney's culture. These priorities must be constantly communicated to ensure the message gets through. He believes that a leader must become a "living, breathing incarnation of your three strategies." Favoring in-person communication, Bob travels extensively. He is determined to relate his organizational priorities and vision to the day-to-day working experience of Disney employees, which he does by continually honing his communication skills.[32]

To change Disney's culture, Bob remade the company through his key priorities, which included the savvy acquisitions we've described. He has been able to preserve the core of Disney while making the company even greater and ensuring it would thrive in this era of constant disruption.

## Thriving After a Fall

There are catastrophes like Elizabeth and Theranos, and then there are other mistakes that are not as disastrous, but also make recovery and re-Thriving difficult—but not impossible.

That was the case for Alex Cora, Puerto Rican native and manager of the Boston Red Sox. It is the story of an otherwise Thriving leader whose lapses in judgment almost cost him a career.

In 2018, Cora was at his peak. After a 16-year playing career as a major league utility infielder, Cora managed in Puerto Rico and worked in broadcasting before being hired as the Houston Astros bench coach in 2017.[34] As the second-in-command to manager A. J. Hinch, Cora helped the team climb to the pinnacle of baseball as they won their first World Series in the team's 60-year history.[35] A year later, Cora was again on the World Series podium, this time with the Red Sox. As a first-time manager, Cora not only took the Red Sox all the way to the World Series but also facilitated a franchise-best season winning record of 108 regular season games.

A little over a year later, he was out of baseball, suspended by Major League Baseball for a year for his role in the Houston Astros sign-stealing cheating scandal.[36] An MLB investigation determined that Cora, while the bench coach for the Houston Astros during the 2017 season, masterminded an illegal sign-stealing system that used live video feeds in the dugout to steal signs, relaying them to batters and base runners through a trash can banging code.[37]

Cora was fired by the Red Sox. The Astros fired general manager Jeff Luhnow and manager A. J. Hinch for their involvement. Carlos Beltran, who had just been announced as the new Mets manager, resigned due to his role as a player in the scheme.[38]

During his year out of baseball, Alex kept a low profile. After the Red Sox had a dismal showing during the 2020 season, the team was again looking for a new manager. While a number of candidates were interviewed, Alex was ultimately rehired. Why? Because Red Sox chief baseball officer Chaim Bloom ultimately came to believe he was the right person for the job.

"Our conversations were lengthy, intense and emotional," Bloom said in a statement released by the Red Sox. "Alex knows what he did was wrong, and he regrets it. My belief is that every candidate should be considered in full: strengths and weaknesses, accomplishments and failures. That is what I did with Alex in making this choice."[39]

While Alex earned the faith of Chaim and the Red Sox, others in the game weren't so sanguine, believing that the Red Sox would achieve a middling record in the 2021 season. Instead, they went on to win the American League East Division Title, defeating two fierce rivals with strong pitching staffs and lineups: the Yankees and the Rays. They came within two games of the World Series, eventually falling to the Astros in the American League Division Championship Series.

No one doubted that Alex was a good baseball manager. His rapport with his players, however, is extraordinary.

"He's a guy you'd run through a wall for," Red Sox reliever Garrett Whitlock said. "If he told me to run through that wall, I'd believe that he had something there to make sure it would fall for me."[40]

"They believe," Chaim said. "In part, because (Cora) believes."[41]

Starting pitcher Eduardo Rodriguez had this to say about Alex: "Like I always say, (Cora's) like a father, brother, manager, whatever. He trusts us. He trusts everybody in that clubhouse. He gives you the chance every time he hands (the ball) to you, and you've just got to go out there and do your job."[42]

For Alex, the playoff wins were sweet not merely because they were wins. After his yearlong suspension for cheating, they were redemption. According to the *Boston Globe*, "Cora has made no secret that he has grown from the pain and shame he caused himself, his family, and others who employed him and who believed in him."[43]

On the field, after the Red Sox beat the Tampa Bay Rays for the American League East Championship, Alex hugged his daughter, Camila, as he wiped away tears. "She suffered a lot, and it was my fault," Alex said. "Sometimes we make bad decisions. And I made a horrible decision in baseball and I paid the price. But what really hurt me was for them to suffer because of my mistakes."[44]

This leads us to one of the most essential traits of a Thriving leader in the world of permanent disruption: the capacity to reflect deeply on one's own leadership shadow and its impact on the world around you. This is especially important in times of setback and failure. Recall from the last chapter that Ray Dalio, author of the bestselling book *Principles: Life and Work*, defines this practice in a simple equation that we refer to often: "Pain + Reflection = Progress."[45] We raise it again because of its simplicity and importance, and to encourage you to keep it in your leader's toolkit wherever you go.

Alex was fortunate that he was able to return to the game he loved, build a successful team, and continue to repair his relationship with his family. Thriving leaders are human. They make mistakes. At their best, Thriving leaders are also humble, with the ability to stay accountable and move on as better, more realized individuals.

In Chapter 8, you'll learn about the Thriving teams of the future and your role in creating them.

## From Insight to Action

**Reflect:** Think about the impact of your leadership and the potential legacy your actions are leading toward. What is the shadow you want to cast and be known for as a leader? What words would you like people to imagine if asked what it's like to work with you?

**Experiment:** Pick one to three of your desired new behaviors and find low-risk opportunities to try them out. What did you learn?

**Choose:** Which of your experiments paid off? Which new behaviors or mindsets will you double down on and which will you let go of?

# CHAPTER 8

# Thriving Teams and Teaming in the Future

A few years back, we conducted an experiment. We were working with an organization that needed to solve a specific business challenge. Within that organization, we put individuals into two different teams to try to solve that problem over a two-day period. Let's call them Team #1 and Team #2.

Team #1 focused on building a Thriving team dynamic on the first day. That involved specific teaming exercises designed to build trust, create a common operating system, gain alignment on a unifying purpose, and develop a growth mindset. They tackled the problem itself on the second day.

Team #2 dove straight into the problem without any teaming exercises.

By the middle of the second day, Team #1 had collectively designed a great solution to the problem. In contrast, Team #2 was still working through the details of their solution as the experiment concluded at the end of the second day.

With this simple experiment—and a number of reconfirming experiments—our team and the organization found the answer to the question of how culture impacts teams. With the right investment, Thriving teams make better, faster decisions than non-Thriving teams.

Unfortunately, all too often, the investment over time in creating and nurturing a Thriving team is a second, third, or fourth thought. Those activities are crammed in at the end of a long off-site meeting. You know it's time to do some team building when everyone's suitcases are lined up at the edge of the conference room! Attention begins to drift away from the exercises to important decisions such as the right time to request the Uber to the airport.

By then, the ship has sailed—it's too late, because not only has the "real" work already been completed, but everyone is mentally and emotionally checked out. They are transitioning away from the team meeting to their jobs and their lives back home. They're tired and, essentially, they're *done*. Despite the lip service that the organization and the leader pay to these team-building activities—claiming that they're important—they are actually not, and everyone knows it.

Our research reveals that just as a car needs an engine or battery to move forward, teams need shared ambitions, purpose, challenges, connection, and commitments. Without that glue to hold the team together, there is no team. Instead, there is a collection of executives who happen to work for the same company. In fact, that's a core belief of a significant percentage of teams when we begin to work with them—instead of a functioning team, they are a group of people who run a business and periodically come together to update each other and make decisions.

The above experiment matches well with the data we're collecting today. Culture Accelerators get culture right first and then deliver outsized results. Today's era of constant disruption requires leaders who understand the importance of investment in teams and teaming, and who are committed to creating cohesive, trusting, aligned teams, not as an afterthought, but as a first move.

In this chapter, we'll explore the stories and qualities of the most successful teams, and those who fail to make teaming a priority. You'll learn about the ways that organizations face this challenge (or don't), and the consequences that flow from these decisions. And you'll see how foundational diversity is to Thriving teams and Thriving in general.

## Challenges at British Airways

How do you lose your position of industry leadership? Simple: let one or two of the wheels of Thriving fall off. For decades, British Airways (BA), the flagship carrier in the United Kingdom, set the global standard for long-haul flying. As a result, the airline had a highly loyal base of frequent flyers and customers, not just in the United Kingdom, but around the world.

"Back in its heyday, BA was the envy of carriers across the globe and a prize of Britain's travel industry," wrote the UAE's *National News*. "It was so proud of its reputation that its marketing slogan in 1983 was 'The World's Favorite Airline,' which it based on the fact that it flew more passengers than any other carrier. Considered a trailblazer in its field, the airline in its early iteration was hailed for ushering in an era of innovative travel."[1] Originally owned by the British government, BA was fully privatized in 1987.[2] From this foundation, BA revolutionized business-class travel with the flat bed, and became the hallmark for long-haul travels in the 1990s and early 2000s.[3]

But changes in leadership and culture fundamentally altered the fortunes and customer experience of BA. Cost-cutting in response to threats from low-fare European upstarts put the carrier in a reactive mode. In 2016, the BA board hired Alex Cruz as CEO from low-cost Spanish carrier Vueling, which was owned by the same parent company as BA, International Airlines Group. Alex was tasked with modernizing the airline to compete with these budget airlines. During his four-year tenure, BA implemented pricing tiers, removed complimentary food and beverages from short-haul flights, and engaged in disputes with employee unions.[4] Cruz also ordered the removal of bathrooms on some planes designed for short-haul flights to cram in more seats.[5]

In 2019, the airline fell to second-to-last place, ahead of only Ryanair, in UK long-haul airline rankings, based on poor customer service, mass flight cancellations, power outages, a hacking incident, and IT failures.[6] During a period of economic prosperity, when consumers and business travelers were flying more than ever, the airline continued to lose traction with its core constituency of business travelers. In our view, leadership diminished vitality and agility within BA, resulting in a decline in performance.

For the first time in 100 years, airline pilots walked out on September 9 and 10, 2019, striking over pay and working conditions in an era when its parent company was raking in record profits.[7] Just before a second planned work stoppage that December, the company and airline reached a deal that called for pay increases of 11.5 percent over three years and future cost-of-living increases.[8]

The airline's reputation didn't improve during the Covid-19 pandemic, when International Airlines Group threatened to slash wages, fire workers, and force them to reapply for their own jobs.[9] The BBC charged that BA's response to the pandemic "created an atmosphere within the company that staff have described as toxic, and prompted a political backlash."

While all airlines were severely impacted by Covid-19, "what marks BA out is the response to its actions—and the palpable resentment now directed at a brand that once invoked national pride," the BBC continued.

Firing CEO Alex Cruz in October 2020 and replacing him with Sean Doyle, whose previous role was CEO of Aer Lingus, didn't immediately change the dynamic. Staff and customer disenchantment persisted.[10] Fifteen months into his tenure, in January 2022, Sean vowed to improve relationships with customers and staff while rebuilding the airline's premium reputation.[11]

"Putting the premium proposition into the hearts of what we do is going to be key," Sean said in an interview with the *Financial Times*. "We want people to come off a British Airways flight and talk about it as if it's something different."[12]

Many were skeptical, including groups of former BA enthusiasts, who now described themselves as ABBA flyers—Anyone but British Airways—mainly because of pre-pandemic cost cutting.[13] In an effort to placate frequent travelers—specifically, members of the airline's Executive Club loyalty program—Sean wrote an open letter in which he stated: "I'm not seeking to make excuses for what should have gone better. What I am doing is making a personal commitment to you that we will build a better British Airways." As part of that pledge, BA restored free drinks and snacks on short-haul trips for World Traveler economy class flyers.[14] Whether the complete BA experience will change for staff and flyers is open to question. We are rooting for them.

Based on our analysis, we believe that the leadership team's focus on yield and optimizing led them to continue to fight the last war in air travel, which caused them to miss the new air travel game. They lost their innovation and agility, their connection to purpose, and the vitality that set the experience of their service apart. This is down to leadership and culture.

We bet you can think of brand names that have been steadfast leaders in their industry one day and virtually disappeared the next. When companies believe they have arrived in a leadership position, sometimes their growth mindset weakens, causing focus on limited, incremental progress that diminishes competitive advantage.

While bottom-line results can certainly be improved with cost cutting, it's almost never the entire answer. Instead, challenges can be handled the way Airbnb responded to the pandemic, by strategically repositioning in a way that created focus on future growth.

## The Role of Trust in Teams

Trust is a complicated aspect of teams and teaming because the word *trust* means so many different things to the individual members of a team.

Beyond the lack of a shared definition, our collective experience reveals a universal decline in trust as a currency of value in relationships. We've found in our work with teams that trust must be part of a shared language, shared perspectives, and shared operating system. As Ed often says, though people view trust as a fundamental currency in our society, we frequently fail to clarify the exchange rate.

Put simply, we all raise our hands in agreement if asked, "Is trust important?" but if you poll each individual in that room, chances are very good you'll get slightly different answers about what trust means for them. This lack of exploring, understanding, and nurturing trust among teammates negatively impacts the spirit of vitality and connection that is so critical to a team's growth and success.

Beyond the interpersonal level of trust, there is the societal or organizational level to think about as well. Edelman's Trust Barometer, a 22-year annual study that surveys trust and its implications, is very helpful in pinpointing why trust is so critical and what organizations need to do to foster it. As the media and government not only fail to foster trust, but are actually generating distrust, the public is turning to organizations to fill that gap. In fact, the 2022 Trust Barometer revealed that:

- 60 percent of those surveyed choose a place to work based on their values and beliefs.
- 88 percent of institutional investors scrutinize environmental, social, and governmental (ESG) factors at the same level as operations and finance. ESG, a synonym for sustainable investing, prioritizes a management approach beyond profitability.[15]
- 64 percent invest based on their values and beliefs.
- 58 percent buy and share information on brands based on their beliefs and values.[16]

These results suggest that business leaders have a once-in-a-generation opportunity—with a mandate from the public—to reinvigorate the perceived level of trust in our institutions. What does this mean for the future of teams and teaming? It means that, as Dr. Paul Zak, author of *Trust Factor: The Science of Creating High-Performance Companies*, explains, employee productivity and performance are directly related to trust. In fact, organizations with a high trust factor outperform and outproduce organizations with low trust factors.[17]

How then do you create a high-trust organization? Start by listening—not just to your team at your headquarters, but throughout your organization. As you listen to your employees, you can start to share your vision of what trust means in terms of your common company operating system. Ask them for input. Along with sharing that definition of trust, you need to lead with a clear and consistent purpose and priorities designed to execute that purpose. People need to trust that what the organization believes is important (its purpose) is fully aligned with the projects and activities they are asked to lead (its priorities). Organizations that develop and consistently communicate a shared framework on trust, along with purpose and priorities, are positioning themselves to create a high-trust environment.

Always remember that restoring trust can be extremely difficult. It's much more effective to maintain the trust and goodwill you already have, rather than squandering it away and then trying to get it back. Thriving, in action, is a trust builder.

## The Operating System for Thriving Teams

The operating system for Thriving teams exists in the same three dimensions as individual Thriving: purpose, a strong spirit of vitality and connection, and an agility and growth mindset. In terms of purpose, at a minimum, there is an overarching ambition for what the team is contributing to. In other words, even if team members have their own individual ambition, there's a clear connection to how that ambition or purpose ladders up to the goals of the team and the organization. Ideally, organizations should have overall goals with division, department, and functional subgoals that connect with larger goals. That's the concrete or hard side, so to speak. The softer side of the goal would be an overarching purpose such as "making healthcare better" or whatever the specific purpose is for that particular team.

In the absence of a clearly defined purpose or ambition, moving an organization forward gets much harder because everyone retreats to their own individual purpose and what they are trying to do with their own teams. In business, unlike sports, there aren't any championships. To set an overall ambition and purpose, an organization and its leaders must be clear on what a championship or win means to them. This includes not only the typical business metrics such as profits, growth, dividends, and so forth, but also progress on sustainability and community impact. Once you get clear on the overarching purpose, or North Star, you can then drill down to more concrete goals for the entire organization, division, department, and function.

In Figure 8.1, the vertical axis represents the degree of ambition or purpose, while the horizontal axis represents orientation in terms of self or others. Within the figure, there are four states:

- Disconnected
- Transactional
- Egocentric
- Thriving

**FIGURE 8.1** Assessing Your Team's Ambition and Orientation

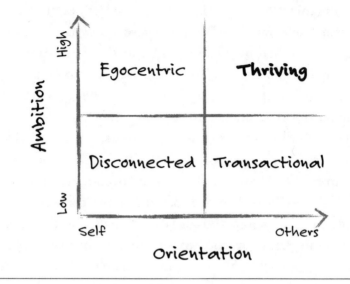

Teams that are self-interested and low on ambition (Disconnected) are not going to thrive because they lack in the dimension of purpose, and they aren't focused enough on others to learn new things in the changing context around them. Maybe they don't even feel that they need to engage in learning.

Teams that are high on ambition and more self-oriented (Egocentric) have multiple ambitious people, each pulling in their own direction, optimizing the pie for themselves. Unfortunately, there is often little focus on the collective potential of the team, causing their energy and focus to diffuse. Alternatively, teams that are high on external focus with low ambition (Transactional) will maintain connection to the pulse of their markets and customers but in a more tactical and incremental fashion, never quite reaching beyond their comfort zone to capture growth. Both Egocentric and Transactional teams may feel to those who are part of them like they're paddling harder to stay in place.

As a simple correlation, we have found that teams that share a strong enterprise-wide ambition or purpose and are externally focused on adapting to the changing world around them are far more likely to thrive. Put simply, these teams think big, boldly, and collectively, and are laser-focused on the markets they serve. The sky's the limit for these teams, and they are typically thrilling to be part of.

Today's world is far too complex for monochromatic teams—in other words, teams that think in one set way. The research revealed that 48 percent of Culture Accelerator CEOs put diversity, equity, and inclusion efforts front and center, compared to 30 percent of other CEOs.[18] Teams require diversity, which ties into a sense of vitality and an expanded purpose or ambition. That includes diversity of thought, diversity of experience, and diversity of background. When the challenges you're facing are highly complex, diversity makes the difference. Diversity also creates the positive conflict necessary for internal team Thriving.

Many groups call themselves a team because they like each other, but when you dig below the surface, some fail to tackle the organization's biggest challenges because they are conflict avoidant and want to keep a "nice" atmosphere. This shallow level of relationship doesn't facilitate the deep connections and trust necessary for Thriving. In this case, having a shared purpose helps to depersonalize constructive feedback and gives an external motivation for having more honest exchanges. The team's work is in service of their purpose, not each other's egos.

Through positive, productive conflict, individual opinions can be tested through a lens of curiosity and agility, and decisions are refined in service of the bigger purpose. To get there, each person on the team prepares to support and defend their position, as well as to be persuaded by the positions of others. From this kind of healthy dynamic comes agility and a more effective level of decision-making.

Ed recalls one former GE executive, who was also a decorated military veteran, telling him bluntly: "The highest-performing teams I've been part of through my career have all been diverse by every measure."

In addition, we have found that Thriving teams work to cultivate a high level of foresight, which we mentioned as part of our deep dive into agility. They anticipate fast-changing trends, shifts in consumer behavior and market conditions, and new ways to create value. And they dedicate time to socializing their learning with each other in hopes of leveling up the entire team.

## Thriving Teams Keep the Bigger Game in Mind

Thriving teams fundamentally understand that what they and their organization are building is not just for them, but also for future generations. That doesn't mean that they don't seek to produce specific near-term results. They do. But in the course of their work, the overall purpose that inspires them into action is timeless and evergreen.

CVS's purpose is a powerful example: "We help people with their health wherever and whenever they need us. And we do it with heart. Because our passion is our purpose: Bringing our heart to every moment of your health."[19]

Let's unpack that. In promising to meet their customers' healthcare needs where they are, CVS creates a partnership with their customers. They further that by linking their purpose and promise with their passion, which is to bring a caring spirit—or heart—into the care they provide. This purpose doesn't limit the company in any way, which leaves it free to change how it fulfills its purpose over time. That's necessary because there is no way to know how healthcare will be delivered in the future. By partnering with their customers without tying themselves down to a specific delivery method, CVS hits the sweet spot of an inspiring and adaptable corporate purpose.

We love this quote from Nelson Henderson about the timeless nature of purpose: "The true meaning of life is to plant trees under whose shade you do not expect to sit."[20]

You may remember from an earlier story how former CVS CEO Larry Merlo sacrificed $2 billion in annual sales by removing cigarettes from all CVS stores in September 2014 and the positive impact that had on smoking rates.[21] "When we removed tobacco from our shelves, a significant number of our customers simply stopped buying and hopefully smoking cigarettes altogether instead of just altering their cigarette purchasing habits," Dr. Troyen Brennan, CVS Health chief medical officer, reported. "This research proves that our decision had a powerful public health impact by disrupting access to cigarettes and helping more of our customers on their path to better health."[22]

Thriving leaders can more easily draw Thriving out of individuals on their teams. Like the leaven in bread, great teams raise each other up and change the game. Thriving teams have no room for executives or individuals driven by ego and self-interest. This doesn't mean that they can't be ambitious. But they're ambitious for the team and the organization first, and themselves second. Later in this chapter, we'll offer some thoughts on the top team killers. Spoiler alert: ego and self-interest are big culprits.

From a shared team reality, committed leadership grows over time. In today's world, most leaders don't know how to think about "Thriving teams," so they can be quick to reject the notion of authentic, impactful team building because it seems touchy-feely and divorced from business outcomes. However, we know that this couldn't be further from the truth. Remember—any competitor can copy most strategies, products, process, and organizational design. Impactful team building—with a focus on creating a cohesive culture—is the secret sauce, the essential ingredient for Thriving organizations in a world of constant disruption.

The Thriving construct is designed to bridge the gap between where most teams are today and where they need to be for tomorrow. When you understand that you and your team can be even more effective when you put team building first—and prioritize that over other objectives on an ongoing basis—you've created the space for a Thriving team and a Thriving organization.

## Toss the Status Quo from Your Team Meetings

To achieve Thriving with a team, the status quo meetings need to get the heave-ho. No more sitting in a circle watching each executive perform an information dump for the CEO. No more tacit agreements that you won't ask tough questions about my presentation and results—as long as I do the same for you. The Thriving teams of the future minimize information dumps and maximize supportive interactions and decision-making.

What might that look like? Move information sharing to email and a company dashboard. Then, use precious meeting time to engage the executive team with common goals that cut across all business lines for constructive debates and decision-making. The lion's share of energy in team meetings should be focused on helping the executive team members work together to drive growth in the business. This approach creates the shared ambition that they're going to learn through. They will gain a sense of connectedness through understanding each other's problems and how they overlap, and working through them together.

As mentioned above, just spending time together doesn't cut it. What you do during that time makes all the difference. Ed recently worked with a leader at a US nationwide retailer who placed such a priority on his executive team spending time together that he held weekly four-hour meetings with the entire team. The first part of the meeting was the usual information dump from each executive before moving on to shared challenges and urgent topics. However, the team felt so exhausted by these weekly ordeals that they were reluctant to speak up about their shared challenges lest they prolong the agony.

The first part of Ed's guidance was to cut out the information dump and find a way to ensure that critical data was shared before the meeting. The second part was for the leader to thoughtfully curate challenges for the team to debate or make decisions on that would foster the three aspects of Thriving. By cutting the meeting down from four hours to two and carefully curating the challenges, the leader and executives all felt an increased sense of energy and purpose. They were able to help each other much more effectively and became increasingly committed to each other's success.

This story demonstrates that a passion for team building and spending time together isn't enough. Instead, team building must be skillful. All too many executives have been burned by clumsy attempts at teaming that waste time and fail to generate results. That's why it's so important to understand the elements crucial to team building and how to gain alignment from your team—and your leaders—before you start.

## Team Killers

Team killers are behaviors that destroy team unity and functionality. While there are many team killers, we'll focus on what we and our clients have identified as the top of the list:

1. Triangulation
2. Cliques
3. Disowning shared commitments
4. Hub-and-spoke structure
5. Tolerating bad behavior

As we've stressed, for teams to function at a Thriving level, they must share many things: trust, commitment, and above all, a common operating system. These five team killers undermine the shared team framework, making positive teaming and Thriving impossible.

### #1: Triangulation

Triangulation—or engaging in three-way conversations—is a team killer because it directly erodes trust between team members. What exactly is triangulation? It's a situation in which one team member challenges or criticizes another team member to a third team member. In other words, if Dustin has an issue with Ed, Dustin chooses to complain to someone else about Ed, instead of having a direct, honest conversation with Ed himself. Why is this bad? Because the whole time Dustin is talking to the third party about Ed, the third party—let's call her Anne—is wondering what Dustin says to others about her when she isn't around. It also undercuts the spirit of unity by driving wedges between people on the team. Instead, keep it real, direct, and honest whenever you encounter interpersonal challenges within your team. Demand that everyone within the team show other team members this type of basic respect. This might sound like an elementary team killer, yet it happens all the time.

## #2: Cliques

The formation of in-groups, or cliques, is directly related to tri-angulation. As a species, humans—particularly primates—are tribally oriented. When you create a tribe, you essentially create an in-group and an out-group. We have a horrible history as human beings of engaging in this behavior. If your team has in-groups and out-groups, teams within teams, cliques within cliques, you end up with people who are officially on the team, but are really part of an out-group. They'll know it, and the entire team will suffer for it. Cliques foster a lack of trust, connection, and transparency, all of which are lethal to team Thriving.

## #3: Disowning Shared Commitments

Ed works with a utility company that experienced a difficult teaming challenge regarding shared commitments. With climate change effects and a movement toward renewable energy, this team made a collective, painful decision about legacy assets that had a profound impact on certain divisions, employees, and stakeholders. Rather than present a united front in the face of this difficult decision, when questioned about the move by some upset employees, several executives broke ranks and disowned involvement in the decision, blaming the CEO and a few team members who "pushed" for the change. Their unwillingness to own this shared decision created even more hard feelings and division down through the organization to the front lines than the actual decision itself did.

David Novak, the original CEO at Yum! Brands, exemplified successful teaming, coining a powerful phrase: team together/team apart. Team members understood that functioning well together when they were in the same room was just part of the challenge. The second conundrum was the team apart. To thrive, team unity must take precedence over individual comfort. That means if there is a necessary but unpopular decision coming from the CEO or another team member, every executive on the management team must back up their teammate immediately and continually, in public and in private. No individual on the team can be allowed to undermine that unity within their own circle or business unit. Assuming the team had an opportunity to deliberate and align to the decision before it was made and announced, everyone has to own the decision with conviction.

## #4: Hub-and-Spoke Structure

Hub-and-spoke structures occur when leaders go out and talk privately with one of their team members, to the exclusion of others, and those two people make an agreement or a decision without input from other affected parties. Typically, these are decisions that should be discussed by a larger, more inclusive group or even made by the team together, collectively. In a hub-and-spoke structure, however, the leader goes out and talks to each team member individually, aggregates their input, and makes a move, without each team member understanding the bigger picture of input. Each time those conversations occur, a new agreement is made that supersedes the previous agreement. By the time the leader has talked to everyone on the team, the leader has had a lot of conversations and gotten a lot of input. The leader then renders a decision that may have very little to do with the substance of what the leader and individual team members actually agreed upon.

This team killer lacks transparency and keeps power concentrated with the leader at the expense of the rest of the team. In addition, this team leadership style gives immediate rise to triangulation, cliques, and disowning of results.

## #5: Tolerating Bad Behavior

Many have seen this situation: an executive who is a top producer or rainmaker lands the big deals, but also behaves atrociously to everyone on the team. Rudeness, profanity, and power trips can be part of this dynamic. And because the executive delivers a powerful bottom-line impact to the company, the leader, or leaders, permit the bad behavior to continue. And as the poorly behaving high-performer realizes that they have a get-out-of-jail-free card, the bad behavior escalates. Finally, something tips it over the edge, up to and including legal liabilities or scandals, and the perpetrator is ultimately fired. Actually, in some cases, the leader gets fired first, due to poor team performance, and the perpetrator continues on, wreaking havoc.

All of this could have been avoided if the leader had taken a hard line on the bad behavior from the beginning. Either the poorly behaving exec would have scaled back due to the boundaries set by the leader, or they would have gotten fired. Ask any leader who has lived through such a traumatic event—they all strongly advise others to become guardians of the team culture, intervene quickly when something is askew, and make essential changes much faster to avoid their mistakes.

## The Future of Teams: Agile Teaming

As organizations continue to evolve in the post-pandemic work environment, they are learning that they must demonstrate flexibility to attract and keep the best talent. Currently, that sometimes means hybrid arrangements where employees work from home a certain number of days a week and go into the office on other days. Some organizations are turning to a team-based decision level on what days will be at home and what days will be in the office. In other words, teams decide what they need and create their optimal schedule accordingly. Many believe the next frontier in workplace flexibility is scheduling flexibility, where employees are given more agency over when they work within an individual workday.

A by-product of the Covid-19 pandemic, the trend toward greater workplace and scheduling flexibility is showing no signs of going away. A 2022 survey of knowledge workers by messaging platform Slack revealed that 95 percent of those polled sought schedule flexibility, which outpolled location flexibility in terms of desirability.[23]

This dyad of flexibility—location and time—is about to be joined by fluidity. In other words, first, organizations create a common operating system and common levels of understanding. Then they build a structure of fluid teams that form, dissolve, re-form, and work across organizational lines as needed.

In today's environment of continual disruption, the life span of an individual team is growing shorter and shorter. CEOs no longer have the luxury of spending a couple of years getting a team to gel and then sitting back and letting them do their thing. While many leaders are adept at developing a team and creating cohesiveness, they are less adept at what we see as the future of teams. Call it agile teaming, where organizations can select the best individuals for a specific task or goal from inside and outside the organization. Once the goal or task is accomplished, those individuals can move on to other teams, tasks, and objectives.

When everything around you is moving, your organization needs to keep moving. Imagine an organization where everyone has a shared language, lexicon, and principles along with trust, connection, growth, agility, purpose, and clarity. These individuals aren't siloed in a specific department or saddled with a specific job function. Instead, they act as a bank of talent that the organization can draw on to accomplish its shared purpose and goals. Such an organization will require Thriving leaders, employees, and teams to function at an optimal level. While this future hasn't been fully realized today, it isn't a fantasy. Instead, it is a reality that could occur sooner than any of us realize.

Now that you understand where the future of teams and teaming is headed, let's move on to the final chapter in our journey together—leveraging Thriving to create a legacy for you and your organization. In this chapter, we make the case for bringing legacy building to the top of your leadership priority list.

## From Insight to Action

**Reflect:** Using the team assessment chart, where would you place the various teams you are part of and/or lead? What one shift would help each team move closer to a Thriving state?

**Experiment:** At your next meeting or team interaction, what is one action you can take to encourage team members in a more positive direction?

**Choose:** Which of the "team killers" will you commit to discouraging or eliminating to ensure more positive, healthy teaming?

# CHAPTER 9

# Crafting a Legacy of Thriving

There's a common thread in our work with C-suite leaders across the globe. As they approach the end of their careers, they increasingly consider their legacy.

"What will I leave behind?" they wonder.

Certainly, we do meaningful work with leaders around this question. But as you near the end of this book, our message to you is—don't wait. Each of us, if we're lucky, lives for roughly 650,000 hours. If you're well into your career, and if you take out sleep, holidays, and weekends, then you have 30,000 to 100,000 hours left for setting that legacy. Seem like a lot? It isn't.

The time to build your legacy—and a better world—is now.

This book was born from our unwavering belief that leaders today can shift the zeitgeist and collectively leave a better world for our kids and all future generations. Not only do better companies deliver better financial outcomes, but they also have the potential to create better futures for people and the planet.

While no one would confuse us for physicists, science provides a helpful analogy. Thriving works because it taps into our very being, the fundamental nature of matter. On a subatomic level, atoms combine three basic components, all with different charges: the proton with a positive charge, a neutron with a neutral charge, and the electron with a negative charge. The dynamic between these three particles underlies everything.

Translating that to Thriving, there are the separate and individual charges of purpose, vitality, and agility. They are all different, but together they create a synergy that elevates individuals, teams, and organizations to function at their highest and best levels. As we've shown in previous chapters, these three must function together to enable Thriving.

In this chapter, we'll demonstrate how this synergy can inform your legacy. Essentially, your legacy is Thriving, scaled.

This chapter provides observations, case studies, and proofs of concept designed to help you start this process whoever you are, wherever you are, regardless of your title or function.

## The Evolution of a Thriving Leader

In the early 1980s, Larry Fink envisioned himself in the CEO's chair at the First Boston Company, a New York City–based investment bank.[1] Hired in 1976 at age 23, Larry got his feet wet trading bonds.[2] At the time, the bond market was the province of institutions and corporations, considered staid and sleepy in comparison to the stock market.[3]

A background in real estate positioned Larry well for a job trading mortgage-backed bonds. Within two years, he was running the department.[4] Within three years, he dove into the new business of structuring and trading securities, including mortgages, car loans, and credit card debt.[5] In fact, Larry was one of the chief innovators in the structured finance market, which today involves the issuance of more than $1 trillion in securities per year globally.[6]

As his career trajectory skyrocketed with the help of an on-fire growth mindset, Larry also developed an aptitude for management. He built a tight-knit team, which added $1 billion to the company's bottom line over time.[7] Recognizing his drive, creativity, and talent, his bosses quickly promoted him, making him the youngest managing director in First Boston's history; soon after, he became the youngest member of the organization's management committee.[8]

"My team and I felt like rock stars," Larry said in a *Vanity Fair* interview. "Management loved us. I was on track to become CEO of the firm. And then . . . well, I screwed up. And it was bad."[9]

Misjudging the direction of interest rates, his bond trading desk lost approximately $100 million when rates fell in 1986. The hedging strategies designed to protect the firm broke down, leading to this shocking loss.[10] Larry eventually left the firm in 1988.[11]

Like all leaders, Larry had a choice of what to do with this painful crucible experience. He chose to take the Thriving path of reflecting deeply on the lessons learned.

In retrospect, he categorized that debacle as a failure of the risk management systems that existed at the time. "We built this giant machine, and it was making a lot of money—until it didn't," Larry told *Vanity Fair* in an extensive series of interviews in 2010. "We didn't know why we were making so much money. We didn't have the risk tools to understand that risk."[12]

Larry decided that he wanted more control over his destiny and the risks that he and his clients would be taking. That meant founding and building an organization that would make money while providing robust risk management tools.[13]

BlackRock was born.

From modest beginnings in a back-room office at private equity firm Blackstone, BlackRock went public 11 years later, in 1999.[14] Today, BlackRock holds $10 trillion in assets under management, which ranks it as the largest global asset management firm.[15]

Not only did Larry succeed in creating the transparent financial powerhouse that he had imagined back in the day when he was smarting from his failure at First Boston, he also oversaw the creation of one of the financial services industry's most comprehensive and powerful risk management platforms, Aladdin. This tool is so valuable and prolific that it is used by rival firms and was even leveraged by the U.S. Treasury department during the global financial crisis of 2007–2009. The execution of this vision made Larry a very wealthy man. In 2021, BlackRock compensated Larry to the tune of $36 million.[16] Forbes estimated his net worth in April 2022 at $1 billion.[17]

For the typical Thriving leader, the size of their bank account is merely a signpost along a much longer and more meaningful journey. For Larry, it is no different. As he matured in his role as BlackRock CEO, he evolved as a leader, his horizons expanded, and his sense of purpose extended well beyond the building of a powerful firm.

He realized the potential he and his organization had to create a meaningful legacy. And he acted upon that, leveraging his position and platform to advance critical issues for society, such as climate change mitigation and the ability of corporations to grow profits through purpose.

One clue that Larry's sense of purpose was expanding was the letters he began to write in 2012—letters to CEOs. Which CEOs? All of them. And because he was the CEO and founder of one of the largest and most influential financial services firms, those CEOs listened. These letters became a widely read platform for Larry to discuss what he viewed as the most critical issues of the day.

To those who know Larry, that shift wasn't a surprise. "There's no hidden agenda with Larry," Ken Langone, founder of Home Depot, told *Vanity Fair* in 2010. "He's right out front. He doesn't run for the hills like some other so-called business leaders."[18]

His first letter was modest in size and scope, informing CEOs about BlackRock's approach to corporate governances and responsible investing in light of the organization's significant influence in voting corporate proxies.[19] In subsequent years, he tackled a number of issues, including:

- The negative impact of Wall Street's short-term focus[20]
- The negative impact of the government's short-term focus
- The ability of corporate sustainability practices to optimize risk-adjusted returns[21]
- The necessity for corporations to embrace net zero targets to reduce global warming[22]

The most recent letter as we completed this book, in 2022, pulled those themes together as a description of capitalism at its best—what he describes as "stakeholder capitalism."[23] This concept places the onus on CEOs and their organizations to act as responsible stewards of capital.

"I believe in capitalism's ability to help individuals achieve better futures, to drive innovation, to build resilient economies, and to solve some of our most intractable challenges," he wrote. "Capital markets have allowed companies and countries to flourish. But access to capital is not a right. It is a privilege. And the duty to attract that capital in a responsible and sustainable way lies with you."

Later in that same letter, he continued, "Our conviction at BlackRock is that companies perform better when they are deliberate about their role in society and act in the interests of their employees, customers, communities, and their shareholders."

Finally, he concluded: "If you stay true to your company's purpose and focus on the long term, while adapting to this new world around us, you will deliver durable returns for shareholders and help realize the power of capitalism for all."[24]

We couldn't provide a more succinct and fitting definition of the Thriving mindset and its potential for positive impact.

## Permission to Think Big

Whether you realize it or not, CEOs, entrepreneurs, and business leaders are uniquely positioned to create broad-based impact. Despite a widespread societal breakdown in trust, CEOs and corporations are among the most trusted individuals and organizations. This trust, revealed in survey after survey, provides CEOs with the platform they need to craft an ambitious legacy.

When contemplating Larry Fink's legacy, for example, it's clear that his influence is built on the vast reservoir of trust he's earned over time within the corporate community. Without that trust, he wouldn't have been inspired to write his series of letters because there would have been no audience, and hence, no point. Instead, Larry intuitively understood that his success at BlackRock created a foundation that he could leverage for a wider purpose.

Trust is a continual theme in this book because without trust there can be no Thriving. Here, we want to reinforce it briefly because it highlights the opportunities and challenges you face in embracing a wider role and crafting a meaningful legacy.

The 2022 Edelman Trust Barometer identified corporations as the most trusted institution in America.[25] This finding is backed up by a PricewaterhouseCoopers (PwC) study that found nearly two-thirds of consumers trust US companies.[26]

Harvard Business School, PwC, and other authoritative sources identify the potential for both good and harm that this high level of trust brings. Companies that raise wages, focus on inclusion, and take actions designed to lower climate impact will solidify that trust, which will accrete to their brands, boosting sales.[27] In fact, the PwC survey revealed that half of consumers surveyed either started buying from particular brands or bought more from brands based on the trust factor.[28]

However, companies that break that trust with data breaches, attempts to cover up mistakes, unethical business practices, and poor treatment of employees are likely to experience a backlash. The PwC survey found that on the flip side, 44 percent of those surveyed stopped buying from a brand due to lack of trust. In addition, 22 percent quit their jobs due to a breach in trust, while 19 percent accepted jobs at organizations that they trusted.[29]

The takeaway from these findings is that leaders with trust in the bank can not only steer business performance to an even higher level, but they can also expand their impact to benefit a much broader set of stakeholders. In other words, your stakeholders—the public, your employees, your customers, and your peers—have given you permission to think big when it comes to legacy.

There is much written about trust, how it's created, and the impact it has. The trust that the corporate world has earned is a valuable commodity that other institutions have squandered. While trust is never bulletproof, we've found the trust intrinsic to Thriving grows from a deeply solid foundation. In other words, leaders who we identify as Thriving are more inherently trustworthy—as perceived by others—than non-Thriving leaders, precisely because of the nature of Thriving. Our research and experiences reveal that a focus on Thriving ensures that you grow trust organically. Why? Because you naturally become a leader who:

- **Creates space for conversations involving empathy and inclusion:** Here, we refer back to the deepest level of listening—listening to your stakeholders with a willingness to be persuaded.
- **Utilizes purpose as a true north:** At its heart, Thriving is about purpose, which at its highest level includes agility and connection.
- **Establishes clear and consistent priorities:** Our research found that the biggest performance and trust derailers are an inability to prioritize that comes from the top.[30]

In one of the most disrupted eras ever, trust is the currency that will see you through no matter what happens. The three principles of Thriving, lived authentically, become a generator of trust. From that position, so much more is possible.

## How to Build Your Legacy

If you're considering your legacy now, we recommend that you work backward from the ultimate impact that you want to achieve. For those of you who are currently CEOs or aspire to become CEOs, you need to understand that you, as the leader, possess a massive amount of influence beyond what you realize. You will leave a legacy, no matter what. The question to ask yourself is, what type of legacy do I want?

Like Larry, if you play a bigger game and are thinking long-term, you can more naturally focus beyond satisfying your shareholders and achieving short-term corporate profits. To expand your vision, consider how you can leverage the platform and your business model or models to achieve maximum impact.

Remember, your potential to create positive impact in the world far exceeds the today and tomorrow that you're given. Think about the potential influence you could have on future generations. This is a level of insight that a Thriving leader can uniquely bring, and it's well within your power to achieve that. Following are three examples of how to expand your purpose to create a legacy of Thriving: through relationships, impact, and preparing the next generation.

## Building a Legacy of Relationships

For General Joe Robles, retired CEO of insurer USAA, placing relationships at the center of the member experience meant understanding what their members were going through and what USAA could do to help. While that may sound trite, for an organization that is based on serving members of the military and their families, a deep exploration of what this concept actually meant to their members was key to its success. Solving day-to-day financial problems for millions of members was a highly meaningful legacy for Joe.

"Most companies talk about the customer, and they say they're going to do everything humanly possible within their abilities to please their customers and do what their customer wants," Joe said in a 2015 interview with Oliver Wyman. "But when you see how their operations are geared, when you see how they do business, when you see how they have their processes laid out, it's anything but centric to the customer, it is generally enterprise or company-centric."[31]

For Joe, ensuring that USAA was truly locked in on customer needs meant flipping the traditional script. How? "At

USAA, we were so used to, for many years, making decisions based on what we thought was best for members, but also what was best for the organization," he explained. "I said, let's clean the slate and let's focus almost totally on how do we make the member happy. How do we make them loyal? How do we make them never want to leave us? How do we change our whole approach and build that relationship that we've talked about?"[32]

Based on this research, the organization built operations and products around the life events that customers experienced. In integrating technology, the objective was to enhance the member experience and create opportunities for conversational interactions rather than automated ones. That meant providing member services representatives with the technology and automated tools they needed to spend more time invested in actual conversations with members.[33]

During and beyond Robles's tenure, USAA increased its commitment to employee welfare by increasing minimum pay per hour to $21 during 2021 while adding on-site childcare facilities and increasing childcare reimbursement. The company also rolled out a scholarship program for employee dependents with financial need, implemented a paid leave program for employees caring for sick family members, and added a family support benefit up to $20,000 for adoption, surrogacy, and infertility treatment expenses.[34] USAA also set and achieved goals for hiring veterans and military spouses.

By achieving this realignment toward their customers and investing more in the workforce, USAA achieved a growth rate of 53 percent in members, 43 percent in revenue, 55 percent in products, and 68 percent in net worth during Robles's tenure.[35] That period between 2007 and 2015 encompassed the Great Recession, making this achievement even more remarkable.

Joe credits his and the organization's success to his investment in building a Thriving corporate culture. In a 2012 interview, he said, "I am the Chief Culture Officer. I make sure that the tone I set and the culture that I reinforce and push is something that will be perpetual and is right for our members and our employees."[36] Building on USAA's six cultural pillars, known as "My Commitment to Service," Joe ensured that new and current employees were grounded in a culture focused on the organization's purpose and values.

## Building a Legacy of Impact

Throughout this book, extreme disruption has been a major theme. The ascendency of social media and the 24-hour news cycle is one major factor that differentiates our experience today from disrupted eras of the past. Axios, a news organization founded in 2017, seeks to counter the fragmentation of society generated by sensationalistic opinion-mongering with its focus on evidence-based journalism. The company defines its purpose as: "Axios gets you smarter, faster on what matters."[37]

After establishing a reputation for solid coverage of national issues, Axios turned its ambitions toward local news. That's a gap that needs filling due to the expanding presence of news deserts. What's a news desert? "A community, either rural or urban, with limited access to the sort of credible and comprehensive news and information that feeds democracy at the grassroots level," according to the University of North Carolina's Hussman School of Journalism and Media's Center for Innovation and Sustainability in Local Media.[38]

You may believe that the innumerable cable and streaming news channels, along with thousands of news websites, have filled this gap. Unfortunately, most cannot fill the shoes of the 360 newspapers that closed during the Covid-19 pandemic.[39] The pandemic aggravated a trend that was already underway in local journalism: American communities have lost more than

25 percent of their newspapers since 2005, leaving 70 million Americans with either no news outlet or a news outlet at risk of closing.

This trend, reported on by Northwestern University Medill School of Journalism, Media, Integrated Marketing Communications' Local News Initiative, puts democracy itself at risk. "This is a crisis for our democracy and for our society," said report author Penelope Muse Abernathy. "Invariably, the economically struggling traditionally underserved communities that need local journalism the most are the very places where it is most difficult to sustain print or digital news organizations."[40]

In fact, as the presence of local news organizations declines in a community, voter participation falls and corruption rises. These factors, according to Abernathy, contribute to "the spread of misinformation, political polarization and reduced trust in the media."[41]

Local news is a challenging market for news organizations, requiring investment in communities of differing sizes, in different regions, and with different challenges. Patch, one of the most ambitious local news undertakings, failed after AOL acquired it and rapidly expanded it to more than 800 local markets. The *Columbia Journalism Review* attributed the failure to uneven quality and lack of profitability.[42]

Axios's launch and expansion efforts in local news have been more measured. By the end of 2021, its 14 local news markets boasted 500,000 subscribers. With some initial success, the company broadened its reach to 11 additional cities. The organization's avowed goals in local reporting include the delivery of original reporting, scoops, and local coverage and curation of the best local reporting, all filtered through the company's trademarked smart brevity style and newsletter format.

Local news is how Axios is furthering its mission on the micro level. On the macro level, Axios is championing capitalism in a similar fashion to Larry Fink. The company's CEO, Jim VandeHei, advocates for what he terms "aspirational capitalism." This embodies four aspects:

1. Aspirational products that solve problems or ease pain points
2. Aspirational longevity that outlasts corporate founders and ephemeral products and services
3. Aspirational meaning for executives, managers, and frontline employees
4. Aspirational betterment that makes your organization a better place[43]

Ultimately, VandeHei and Axios champion a new corporate model that prizes sustainability above "wild growth, wild personalities, and wild wealth."[44] We expect more such messages to follow from other CEOs as the rise of the Thriving-minded leader continues.

## Building a Legacy by Preparing the Next Generation

An important aspect of legacy is preparing the next generation of talent. A great example of this quality is Sipho Maseko, who executed a turnaround at SA Telkom, then handed over the reins to a highly capable successor and an entire next generation of talent.

Prior to his resignation, Sipho carefully nurtured the next generation of leaders. One of those leaders, Serame Taukobong, was ultimately selected to succeed him as group CEO designate.[45] Serame spent the past three years as head of the organization's mobile business, which doubled in value during his tenure. Previously, he worked at one of Telkom's major competitors serving in a variety of operational, sales, marketing, and supervision roles in Iran, South Africa, and Ghana. Initially,

South African financial markets reacted negatively to Sipho's departure, but they recovered when Serame's appointment was announced.[46]

Sipho organized his transition extensively and initially planned to stay for a full year to mentor his successor. In an unexpected move, Sipho and the Telkom board decided in January that he would leave six months ahead of his initially announced departure, saying that the "transition process had gone incredibly well." A strong factor in this positive assessment was the expected continuity of business strategy between the two executives.[47] Because the two worked closely together, Serame was well positioned to build on Sipho's success.

## Supersize Your Impact

When we encourage leaders to level up their thinking, it's important to note that we're not talking about activities that are separate from what you're already doing. What we're suggesting is that you put a bigger context around whatever you're doing. In other words, ask, how can you supersize your impact?

Larry Fink's story is a great example. Clearly, he was considering some of these questions at an early phase in his career his departure from First Boston. Over time, he realized that he'd earned an opportunity to influence on a broader scale.

As he allowed his vision to expand, he created new linkages from his business model to the longer-term concerns of the wider world. He didn't just randomly decide to champion certain causes—instead, he realized the importance of these issues to the ultimate flourishing of capitalism, and sought to integrate them. In other words, his business model upgraded to become what we call a purpose model.

The ongoing disruption of this era hasn't stopped Larry. Instead, he's capturing the energy of that disruption, as a consummate surfer, to propel his team, organization, and the world at large forward.

You'll find similar themes in the stories of the other leaders we've highlighted in this chapter. Joe Robles succeeded in placing relationships at the center of USAA, while Sipho Maseko wanted to ensure that his efforts to create a modern African communications infrastructure would continue.

In the final section, we'll leave you with a few concluding thoughts to help you process the content we've provided and integrate it into your life.

## From Insight to Action

**Reflect:** Picture yourself years from now. What legacy do you want to leave? What do you hope people will say about you as a leader, as a person, and about what you've left behind?

**Experiment:** How will you start living your legacy now? What does it look like in action and with whom? What opportunities do you have to experiment with different approaches?

**Choose:** Consider the most important area of your life. What improved outcomes do you want to see—today, in a year, in five to ten years? A year from now, what will you be thrilled that you started today as a result of this choice?

# CONCLUSION

# Lead Through Anything

Two years into the American Civil War, the Union's prospects seemed bleak.[1] Both in the east and west, the Union was either losing ground or in a stalemate. Not only did Robert E. Lee's Army of Northern Virginia decisively defeat a much larger Army of the Potomac at Chancellorsville in May 1863, but the Confederate Army continued to hold off Union armies at Vicksburg, Mississippi, that sought to divide the rebels geographically.[2]

Within the Union, unity was fracturing. The preliminary Emancipation Proclamation had proven divisive as antiwar Democrats, midwestern separatists, and others roiled Lincoln's coalition.[3] Personally, Abraham Lincoln and his wife, Mary Todd Lincoln, were grieving over the loss of their 11-year-old son, Willie, who died in 1862 in the White House.[4] Not only did Lincoln have to wrestle with his own depression and health issues, but he also had to contend with Mary's compulsive shopping habits, emotional instability, and explosive temper.[5]

At this point, Lincoln's legacy was far from assured. While today the Union's victory in the Civil War seemed preordained, as it was unfolding, the outcome was far from certain. Such is the case for many historic success stories.

This snapshot in time of Lincoln's life reveals how complex the process of growing into a state of Thriving actually is. There are multiple moving parts, both internally and externally. Yet, clearly, an indomitable spirit and the seeds of greatness existed within Lincoln at that time. Less than two years after the calamitous defeat at Chancellorsville, Lee signed the surrender document at Appomattox Court House on April 9, 1865, ending the Civil War. This action not only preserved the Union, but also established Lincoln's legacy.[6]

Of all the great historical figures throughout time, we hold Lincoln in the highest esteem. He was steadfast in purpose, constantly learning and remaining agile, and had a gift for creating vitality through interpersonal connection and the application of his energy. For us, he exemplifies how Thriving can help you lead through anything and build a better world.

Of the hundreds of business books we've read over the years and the many methodologies we've investigated, there's no other system that we've seen that measures up to the multidimensionality of Thriving. All too many are pegged to the latest trends, offering little value out of context. What excites us and our clients about Thriving is that these principles are the ultimate all-weather business tool. As we continue to develop this methodology, the sky is literally the limit for Thriving itself and the Thriving leaders and organizations of today and tomorrow.

## Backtest These Principles

This is why we've used Lincoln to backtest our principles. As we mentioned early on, backtesting involves applying historical data to test strategies and theories. When we look at Lincoln through the Thriving model of purpose, vitality, and agility, he stands out in the way he built one of the most meaningful and profound legacies in American history despite extreme external and internal disruption.

Yet it's important to note that Thriving isn't a guarantee of happiness in the future, or, in fact, of anything. What Thriving does is provide a space within yourself to be fully grounded despite what's happening in the outside world and within your personal world, so you can learn to lead through anything.

"Most folks are about as happy as they make up their minds to be," is one of Lincoln's most well-known sayings. He exemplifies this quote. While most of us are familiar with his successes—uniting a divided nation by winning the Civil War—not as many are familiar with his political career or personal life. Lincoln lost almost as many elections as he won. Of the four sons that he and Mary Todd Lincoln had, three died during childhood.[7] He sent more than 360,000 Union soldiers to their deaths during the five-year conflict.[8]

The Smithsonian Institution describes Lincoln's legacy in this way:

> *Temperamentally, he was humane, tolerant, and patient. But he also had an extraordinary ability to see events clearly and adapt to them, responding decisively when necessary. Above all, there is his evolution on civil rights. He began the Civil War with thoughts only of restoring the Union, but also ended up committing the nation to freedom for African-Americans.*[9]

Clearly, Abraham Lincoln exceeded the bar of Thriving. In guiding the nation through a period of unprecedented turmoil, he provided a sense of purpose and connection, all while adapting to a continually changing landscape.

We encourage you to backtest these principles by running your role models through the Thriving principles. Don't take our word for it—investigate for yourself. Do you see evidence from each of the three principles? This timeless and time-tested methodology functions as a verification tool for the leaders of today and yesterday.

## Ascending Mountains

In today's ultra-disrupted reality, our personal and professional lives are analogous to climbing an increasingly challenging range of mountains. Since 2007, we've experienced the biggest economic downturn since the Great Depression, a global pandemic that's killed nearly 7 million people and counting worldwide, US inflation spiking to a four-decade high of 8.6 percent, renewed hostilities between the East and West, and a tug-of-war between employers and employees over returning to work.[10]

For those who argue that there have been periods in the past that have been just as disruptive, we agree. The 1970s, for instance, featured the OPEC oil embargo, the Watergate scandal, stagflation, the Vietnam War, and more. Abraham Lincoln faced the breakup of the United States in the 1860s. What's different today is the lightning speed at which information—and disinformation—moves across the globe. No period of history except this one has featured so many disruptive events that have been communicated, twisted, distorted, and magnified in the ways that we are witnessing today.

There's precious little visibility about what's around the next corner for you, your team, and your organization. No wonder many are feeling increasingly frustrated, fatigued, and frazzled. The American Psychological Association reported in early 2022 that burnout and stress are at all-time highs across professions.[11] The World Health Organization defines burnout as "a syndrome . . . resulting from workplace stress that has not been successfully managed. It is characterized by three dimensions: feelings of energy depletion or exhaustion; increased mental distance from one's job, or feelings of negativism or cynicism related to one's job; and reduced professional efficacy."[12]

We believe that Thriving is the antidote for this perpetual burnout, and we've seen it work for leaders around the world. When implemented with leadership alignment and support from the top to the front lines, Thriving works as an organization's operating system and connective tissue. When executives, managers, and employees understand and endorse a guiding purpose, leverage that purpose to grow, and compound those dynamics through a mindset of vitality and connection, the stage is set for success.

When you truly understand your own strengths and challenges and can function with an agile mindset in contrast to a fixed mindset, you have the potential to strike the right balance between purpose, vitality, and agility, which creates and sustains a Thriving state.

What's exciting about this methodology is that it begins with you. Regardless of what internal or external disruptions are occurring, you have the potential to shape your own world. You can create that calm center within yourself that will navigate through whatever storms arise. Thriving, in concert with a deep sense of humility, will help you overcome whatever obstacles are placed in your path.

Regardless of the world's verdict as to your ultimate achievement, if you make the decision to lead a Thriving life, we believe you'll enjoy a more deeply satisfying experience, create and nurture richer relationships, grow yourself and others to increasingly high levels of performance, and generate more sustainable successes over the long term for an expanded network of stakeholders and communities. And, with purpose as your North Star, you'll have done your part to make the world a better place—a world better led.

The world needs your leadership. And we wish you every success along this rewarding journey as you learn to lead through anything.

# AFTERWORD
## By Rose Gailey

Approaching the last chapter of *Lead Through Anything,* an earlier quote by Ed Manfre and Dustin Seale reverberated: *"One of the most essential traits of a Thriving Leader in the world of permanent disruption is the capacity to reflect deeply on one's own leadership shadow and its impact on the world around you."* This is a poignant summary of the book's primary intent: to stimulate, inspire and challenge individual reflection and clarity around the power of purpose, vitality and agility.

As they underscored, *"This book was born from our unwavering belief that leaders today can shift the zeitgeist and collectively leave a better world for our kids and all future generations."* Their passion and commitment to that unwavering belief was evident on every page.

Having spent most of my career helping leaders purposefully shape their organizations' cultures, I know there is great evidence that a resilient leader will inspire a resilient organization. Indeed, a Thriving leader will secure a culture that can thrive amidst, in spite of, and, in fact, because of disruption.

As they remind us, *"To thrive in this era of continual disruption, you must completely take responsibility for your personal leadership shadow and your organization's culture."* The book's invitation to awareness, intention and practice is a formula for successfully taking that personal responsibility as a leader and fostering a Thriving culture.

While the book was set in the context of unrelenting change, Ed and Dustin challenge us to remain future-focused. There are myriad trends that leaders must stay on top of. While the list of potential disruptions is daunting, the reliable course for meeting these present and future challenges is to lead with purpose, vitality and agility.

As Dustin and Ed caution, *"When everything around you is moving, your organization needs to keep moving."* A Thriving leadership stance brings to life the vision they shared which is truly achievable: *"Imagine an organization where everyone has a shared language, lexicon, and principles along with trust, connection, growth, agility, purpose, and clarity."* This vision encompasses the definition of a truly Thriving culture.

Near the end of the book, the topic of legacy comes into focus. Long after completing the final chapter, I continue to contemplate the legacy I want to leave behind as a mother, community member, and leader. I am inspired to delve more deeply into what it means for me to lead a Thriving life, even more significantly marked by purpose, vitality and agility.

As I come to the end of *Lead Through Anything*, I am incredibly grateful to Ed and Dustin, my valued colleagues and friends, for their purpose-driven writing that is sure to inspire leaders to thrive and, in turn, inspire thriving teams, organizations, and communities for years to come.

**Rose Gailey** is the Global Lead and Partner, Organization Acceleration & Culture Shaping at Heidrick Consulting, and coauthor of *Future Focused: Shape Your Culture, Shape Your Future.*

# NOTES

## INTRODUCTION

1. "10 Warren Bennis Quotes on Leadership," iU eMagazine, June 3, 2017, https://www.iuemag.com/u17/di/10-warren-bennis-quotes-on-leadership-in-business.php.
2. Steve, Olenski, "7 Albert Einstein Quotes and What They Mean for CMOs," Oracle, May 13, 2022, https://blogs.oracle.com/marketingcloud/post/7-albert-einstein-quotes-and-what-they-mean-for-cmos.

## CHAPTER 1

1. "Martin Glenn: FA Chief Executive to Leave at End of the Season," BBC.com, Dec. 13, 2018, https://www.bbc.com/sport/football/46553392.
2. Charlotte Carroll, "What Is the Rooney Rule? Explaining the NFL's Diversity Policy for Hiring Coaches," SportsIllustrated.com, Dec. 31, 2018, www.si.com/amp/infl/2018/12/21/rooney-rule-explained-nfl-diversity-policy.
3. Adam Reed, "English Soccer Seeks New Chief Executive, After Martin Glenn Announces He's to Step Aside," CNBC.com, Dec. 13, 2018, https://www.cnbc.com/2018/12/13/fa-chief-executive-martin-glenn-resigns.html.
4. Senn Delaney, "The Power of a Thriving Organization at the Top," Heidrick & Struggles.
5. Gráinne Ní Aodha, PA, "Both Historic and Very Ordinary: The Queen's 2011 Visit to Ireland," *Irish News*, Sept. 8, 2022, https://www.irishnews.com/news/republicofirelandnews/2022/09/08/news/both_historic_and_very_ordinary_the_queen_s_2011_visit_to_ireland-2822512/.

6. Irish War Museum, "What You Need to Know About The Troubles," https://www.iwm.org.uk/history/what-you-need-to-know-about-the-troubles.

7. Ní Aodha, "Both Historic and Very Ordinary."

8. "Queen Elizabeth Remembered in Ireland for Historic Reconciliation," Al Jazeera, Sept. 9, 2022, https://www.aljazeera.com/news/2022/9/9/queen-elizabeth-remembered-in-ireland-for-historic-reconciliation.

9. Alan Cowell, "Queen's Ireland Visit Seen as Significant Advance," *New York Times*, May 20, 2011, https://www.nytimes.com/2011/05/21/world/europe/21queen.html.

10. "Queen Elizabeth Remembered in Ireland."

11. Ní Aodha, "Both Historic and Very Ordinary."

12. Cowell, "Queen's Ireland Visit."

13. "Both historic and very ordinary: the Queen's 2011 visit to Ireland," *Irish News*, Sept. 8, 2022, https://www.irishnews.com/news/republicofirelandnews/2022/09/08/news/both_historic_and_very_ordinary_the_queen_s_2011_visit_to_ireland-2822512/; "Bloody Sunday 90th anniversary commemorated," *The Nationalist*, December 1, 2010, https://archive.ph/20130217191227/http://www.nationalist.ie/news/local/bloody-sunday-90th-anniversary-commemorated-1-2369085.

14. Cowell, "Queen's Ireland Visit."

15. John Hennessy, "Embracing the Need to 'Learn and Relearn," *Stanford Magazine*, January/February 2002, https://stanfordmag.org/contents/embracing-the-need-to-learn-and-relearn.

16. Sharon Terlep, "CVS Boss Larry Merlo's Path from Corner Pharmacy to C-Suite," *Wall Street Journal*, Dec. 5, 2017, https://www.wsj.com/articles/cvs-boss-larry-merlos-path-from-corner-pharmacy-to-c-suite-1512475200.

17. Susan Morse, "Aetna President to Take Helm of CVS Health as CEO Larry Merlo Steps Down Next Year," Nov. 6, 2020, https://www.healthcarefinancenews.com/news/aetna-president-take-helm-cvs-health-ceo-larry-Larry-steps-down.

18. Zoë Henry, "This Business Move Cost CVS $2 Billion (but It Was the Smartest Business Decision It Could Have Made," Inc.com, May 10, 2016, https://www.inc.com/zoe-henry/cvs-lost-2-billion-socially-conscious-business-move.html.

19. Matt Egan, "CVS Banned Tobacco. Now Its Sales Are Hurting," MoneyCNN.com, Aug. 4, 2015, https://money.cnn.com/2015/08 /04/investing/cvs-earnings-cigarettes/.

20. Egan, "CVS Banned Tobacco."

21. Jennifer M. Polinski et al., "Impact of CVS Pharmacy's Discontinuance of Tobacco Sales on Cigarette Purchasing (2012–2014)." *American Journal of Public Health*, April 2017, https://www.ncbi.nlm .nih.gov/pmc/articles/PMC5343689/.

22. "CVS Health Announces CEO Transition Effective February 2021," CVSHealth, Nov. 6, 2020, https://cvshealth.com/news -and-insights/press-releases/cvs-health-announces-ceo-transition -effective-february-2021.

23. "2020 Airbnb Update," Airbnb.com, Jan. 2020, https://news.airbnb .com/2020-update/.

24. "The 21st-Century Corporation: A Conversation with Brian Chesky of Airbnb," mckinsey.com, https://www.mckinsey.com/capabilities /strategy-and-corporate-finance/our-insights/the-21st-century -corporation-a-conversation-with-brian-chesky-of-airbnb.

25. "A Message from Co-Founder and CEO Brian Chesky," Airbnb .com, May 2020, https://news.airbnb.com/a-message-from-co -founder-and-ceo-brian-chesky/.

26. Noor Zainab Hussain and Joshua Franklin, "Airbnb Valuation Surges Past $100 Billion in Biggest U.S. IPO of 2020," Reuters .com, Dec. 2020, https://www.reuters.com/article/airbnb-ipo /airbnb-valuation-surges-past-100-billion-in-biggest-u-s-ipo-of -2020-idUSKBN28K261.

27. "Aligning Culture with the Bottom Line: How Companies Can Accelerate Progress," Heidrick.com, https://www.heidrick.com /en/insights/culture-shaping/aligning-culture-with-the-bottom-line -how-companies-can-accelerate-progress.

## CHAPTER 2

1. "The Telkom Story—from a Dominant Monopoly to Begging for Help," Mybroadband.co.za, Feb. 9, 2020, https://mybroadband .co.za/news/business-telecoms/338008-the-telkom-story-from -a-dominant-monopoly-to-begging-for-help.html.

2. "Factbox: South Africa's Divisive Ex-president Zuma's Many Scandals," Reuters, June 29, 2020, https://www.reuters.com/world/africa/south-africas-divisive-ex-president-zumas-many-scandals-2021-06-29/.

3. Tara Kangarlou, "South Africa Since Apartheid: Boom or Bust?," CNN.com, Nov. 27, 2013, http://edition.cnn.com/2013/11/27/business/south-africa-since-apartheid/index.html.

4. Telkom, "Integrated Report for the Year Ended 31 March 2021," Telkom SA SOC Ltd, https://www.telkom.co.za/ir/apps_static/ir/pdf/financial/pdf/Telkom_Integrated_Report_2021.pdf.

5. "Telkom CEO Sipho Maseko's Legacy," Mybroadband.ca.za, Aug. 19, 2021, https://mybroadband.co.za/news/business/410260-telkom-ceo-sipho-masekos-legacy.html.

6. Senn Delaney, "Creating Better Business Results Through a Thriving State of Mind," Heidrick & Struggles.

7. Julie Riddle, interview with Colin Powell, "Attitude Matters," Whitworth University, Fall 2018, https://www.whitworth.edu/cms/our-stories/magazine/colin-powell/.

8. Telkom, "Integrated Report for the Year Ended 31 March 2021."

9. "Company Profile: Our Strategy Review," South African Telkom, https://www.telkom.co.za/about_us/companyprofile/company-profile.shtml.

10. "CSP Profile: Telkom SA," TelkomTV.com, https://www.telecomtv.com/content/telkom-sa/.

11. "Telkom Now 'Solidly' SA's Number Three Mobile Operator After Covid-19 Bump," BusinessLive.co.za, Nov. 10, 2020, https://www.businesslive.co.za/bd/companies/telecoms-and-technology/2020-11-10-telkom-now-solidly-sas-number-three-mobile-operator-after-covid-19-bump/.

12. Telkom, "Company Profile: Our Strategy Review."

13. "11 Facts About HIV in Africa," DoSomething.org, https://www.dosomething.org/us/facts/11-facts-about-hiv-africa.

14. "An Outlandish Idea That Saves Lives," Dartmouth Campaign, March 18, 2019, https://calltolead.dartmouth.edu/stories/outlandish-idea-saves-lives.

15. "An Outlandish Idea That Saves Lives."

16. "Our Model, Our Impact," GrassrootsSoccer.org, https://grassrootsoccer.org/overview/.

17. Andrew Jack, "Football Charities Face Challenges in Teaching South African Teens about HIV," *Financial Times*, May 3, 2018, https://www.ft.com/content/959343e2-43fb-11e8-97ce-ea0c2bf34a0b.

18. "Join a Grassroots Youth Movement Ignited by Soccer to Eliminate the Adolescent Health Gap," Grassroots Soccer.org, https://grassrootsoccer.org.

19. Mark A. Gabriel, *Visions for a Sustainable Energy Future* (River Publishers/Routledge, 2008), https://www.routledge.com/Visions-for-a-Sustainable-Energy-Future/Gabriel/p/book/9780849398179.

20. "Committed to the Traditions and Principles That Put Members First," unitedpower.com, May 2021, unitedpower.com/mayjune-message-mark-gabriel.

21. McKinsey, "Stay Visible—but Don't Be Needed: How Alain Bejjani Is Leading Through the Unexpected," McKinsey, Aug. 3, 2020, https://www.mckinsey.com/business-functions/strategy-and-corporate-finance/our-insights/stay-visible-but-dont-be-needed-how-alain-bejjani-is-leading-through-the-unexpected.

22. Gelles, "Unilever Finds That Shrinking Its Footprint Is a Giant Task."

23. "First He Saved Unilever. Now He Wants to Save Capitalism," Harvard Business Review IdeaCast, Episode 822, Oct. 05, 2021, https://hbr.org/podcast/2021/10/first-he-saved-unilever-now-he-wants-to-save-capitalism.

24. Rhett A. Butler, "Putting Sustainability at the Center of Business Strategy: An Interview with Paul Polman," Mongabay.com, Oct. 19, 2020, https://news.mongabay.com/2020/10/putting-sustainability-at-the-center-of-business-strategy-an-interview-with-paul-polman/.

25. "Unilever's Purpose-Led Brands Outperform."

26. Butler, "Putting Sustainability at the Center of Business Strategy.

27. "Paul Polman, Co-Founder and Chair Emeritus," Imagine.one, https://imagine.one/paul-polman/.

28. Catherine Zhu, "Interview with Umran Beba, PepsiCo," EgonZehnder, Jan. 1, 2017, https://www.egonzehnder.com/insight/interview-with-umran-beba-pepsico.

29. "PepsiCo Leading the Way in Digital Transformation in HR," TurkofAmerica.com, Jan. 12. 2021, https://turkofamerica.com/index.php/people/professionals/item/4688-pepsico-leading-the-way-in-digital-transformation-in-hr.

## CHAPTER 3

1. Hugh Delehant, "Buddha and the Bulls: An Interview with Phil Jackson," *Tricycle* magazine, Summer 1994, https://tricycle.org /magazine/buddha-and-bulls/.

2. "Phil Jackson," Basketball-Reference.com, Jan. 4, 2022, https://www .basketball-reference.com/players/j/jacksph01.html; "Phil Jackson," Basketball-Reference.com, Jan. 4, 2022, https://www.basketball -reference.com/coaches/jacksph01c.html.

3. Delehant, "Buddha and the Bulls."

4. Delehant, "Buddha and the Bulls."

5. Billy Witz, "Jackson the Iconoclast, Coolly Collecting Rings," *New York Times*, March 15, 2014, https://www.nytimes.com/2014/03/16 /sports/basketball/jackson-the-iconoclast-coolly-collecting-rings .html.

6. Daniel Szewczyk, "Kobe Bryant, Michael Jordan and the 25 Greatest Players to Play for Phil Jackson," TheBleacherReport.com, May 9, 2011, https://bleacherreport.com/articles/690996-25-greatest -players-under-phil-jackson.

7. "List of NBA Championship Head Coaches," Basketball.fandom.com, https://basketball.fandom.com/wiki/List_of_NBA_championship _head_coaches.

8. "Phil Jackson," HoopHall.com, https://www.hoophall.com/hall-of -famers/phil-jackson/.

9. "Bill Belichick by the Numbers: As NFL Legend Turns 69, Patriots Coach Has Opportunity to Rewrite Record Books," CBSSports .com, April 16, 2021, https://www.cbssports.com/nfl/news/bill -belichick-by-the-numbers-as-nfl-legend-turns-69-patriots-coach -has-opportunity-to-rewrite-record-books/.

10. Pete Schauer, "The Best New York Yankees Managers of All Time," BleacherReport.com, Oct. 19, 2011, https://bleacherreport.com /articles/900855-the-best-new-york-yankees-managers-of-all-time.

11. Toe Blake, "9 Best NHL Coaches," ProStackHockey.com, n.d., https://www.prostockhockey.com/hockey-resources/best-nhl -coaches/.

12. Kevin Ding, "In-Depth Breakdown of Phil Jackson's New Book, *Eleven Rings: The Soul of Success*," BleacherReport.com, May 21, 2013, https://bleacherreport.com/articles/1646622-in-depth-breakdown -of-phil-jacksons-new-book-eleven-rings-the-soul-of-success.

13. Mark Schruender, "Five Quotes from Phil Jackson on Focus," Basketballgrowthmindset.com, Nov. 11, 2018, http://basketballgrowthmindset.com/five-quotes-from-phil-jackson-on-focus/.

14. Suneera Tandon, "Saad Abdul-Latif, PepsiCo CEO for AMEA Region, Dies," LiveMint.com, Aug. 20, 2013, https://www.livemint.com/Companies/t7f8GDACLLhKRsAdfVYDgK/Saad-AbdulLatif-PepsiCo-CEO-for-AMEA-region-dies.html.

15. "Reckitt Benckiser: Fast and Focused Innovation," Harvard Business School, May 21, 2011, https://hbsp.harvard.edu/product/311116-PDF-ENG.

16. Rebecca M. Henderson and Ryan Johnson, "Reckitt Benckiser: Fast and Focused Innovation," Harvard Business School, June 1, 2011 (revised May 21, 2012), https://hbsp.harvard.edu/product/311116-PDF-ENG.

17. Henderson and Johnson, "Reckitt Benckiser: Fast and Focused Innovation."

18. Reckitt Benckiser, "Our Focus Is the Key to Our Success," *Business Today* magazine, Dec. 30, 2007, https://www.businesstoday.in/magazine/60-minutes/story/our-focus-is-the-key-to-our-success-12544-2007-12-12.

19. Benckiser, "Our Focus Is the Key to Our Success."

20. Henderson and Johnson, "Reckitt Benckiser: Fast and Focused Innovation."

21. Henderson and Johnson, "Reckitt Benckiser: Fast and Focused Innovation."

22. "Sisyphus," GreekMythology.com, https://www.greekmythology.com/Myths/Mortals/Sisyphus/sisyphus.html.

23. Ihsaan Fanusie, "Former Yum CEO Describes the One Trait All Leaders Have in Common," Yahoo!Finance, Aug. 11, 2021, https://news.yahoo.com/ex-yum-ceo-describes-the-one-trait-all-leaders-have-in-common-172455425.html.

24. Fanusie, "Former YUM CEO Describes the One Trait.

25. CNBC Guest Author Blog, David Novak, January 9, 2012, https://www.cnbc.com/id/45860026#:~:text=If%20you're%20one%20person,About%20the%20author%3A%20David%20C.

## CHAPTER 4

1. Derek Thompson, "Why Steve Ballmer Failed," *Atlantic*, Aug. 23, 2013, https://www.theatlantic.com/business/archive/2013/08/why -steve-ballmer-failed/278986/.

2. Erica Mealy, "Windows XP Turns 20: Microsoft's Rise and Fall Points to One Thing—Don't Fix What Isn't Broken," TheConversation.com, Oct. 24, 2021, https://theconversation.com /windows-xp-turns-20-microsofts-rise-and-fall-points-to-one-thing -dont-fix-what-isnt-broken-166493.

3. "Mealy, Windows XP Turns 20."

4. Kaitlyn Kubrick, "The Star of an Era: The Success Story of Windows XP," SoMagNews.com, https://www.somagnews.com/the -star-of-an-era-the-success-story-of-windows-xp/.

5. Matthew Hughes, "Why Windows XP Won't Be Going Away Anytime Soon," Makeuseof.com, Nov. 1, 2015, https://www.makeuseof .com/tag/windows-xp-wont-going-away-anytime-soon/.

6. Shona Ghosh, "Windows XP Is Still the Third Most Popular Operating System in the World," BusinessInsider.com, May 15, 2017, https://www.businessinsider.com/windows-xp-third-most-popular -operating-system-in-the-world-2017-5.

7. Thompson, "Why Steve Ballmer Failed."

8. Jay Yarrow, "Steve Ballmer's Biggest Mistakes As CEO of Microsoft," Business Insider, Aug. 27, 2013, https://www.businessinsider.com /steve-ballmers-most-epic-mistakes-as-ceo-of-microsoft-2013-8.

9. Jason Hiner, "The Top Five Reasons Why Windows Vista Failed," ZDNet.com, Oct. 5, 2008, https://www.zdnet.com/article/the-top -five-reasons-why-windows-vista-failed/.

10. Nithil Krishnaraj, "Windows Vista: Why Did It Fail?" Medium .com, June 22, 2020, https://medium.com/techtalkers/windows -vista-why-did-it-fail-b3ba4bd08a74.

11. Monica Langley, "Ballmer on Ballmer: His Exit from Microsoft," *Wall Street Journal*, Nov. 17, 2013, https://www.wsj.com/articles/SB1 0001424052702303460004579194150724298162.

12. Langley, "Ballmer on Ballmer."

13. Matt Weinberger, "The Rise of Satya Nadella, the CEO Who Totally Turned Microsoft Around in 5 Years and Made It More

Valuable than Apple," Business Insider.com, Feb. 4, 2019, https://www.businessinsider.com/the-rise-of-microsoft-ceo-satya-nadella-2016-1.

14. Share prices on Google Finance.

15. Richard Beales, "Microsoft and Satya Nadella to Be Tech Standouts," Reuters.com, Jan. 4, 2022, https://www.reuters.com/breakingviews/microsoft-satya-nadella-be-tech-standouts-2022-01-04/.

16. "Satya Nadella Email to Employees on First Day as CEO," Microsoft.com, Feb. 4, 2013, https://news.microsoft.com/2014/02/04/satya-nadella-email-to-employees-on-first-day-as-ceo/.

17. Brett Molina, "Zain Nadella, Son of Microsoft CEO Satya Nadella, Has Died," *USA Today*, March 1, 2022, https://www.usatoday.com/story/tech/2022/03/01/zain-nadella-son-microsoft-ceo-dies/6978789001/.

18. Sandra Jones, "Leadership Lessons from Satya Nadella," *Chicago Booth Magazine*, Jan. 10, 2019, https://www.chicagobooth.edu/magazine/leadership-lessons-satya-nadella.

19. Jones, "Leadership Lessons from Satya Nadella."

20. Sachin Waikar, "Microsoft CEO Satya Nadella: Be Bold and Be Right," Stanford Business, Nov. 26, 2019, https://www.gsb.stanford.edu/insights/microsoft-ceo-satya-nadella-be-bold-be-right.

21. Daniel Howley, "Microsoft Stock Set to Hit $300 as It Becomes 'Cloud Behemoth,' Analyst Says," Yahoo!Finance, Oct. 27, 2021, https://news.yahoo.com/microsoft-stock-set-to-hit-400-as-it-becomes-cloud-behemoth-analyst-says-141608286.html.

22. "Martin Glenn: Mr Can Do," *The Independent*, Aug. 22, 2005, https://www.independent.co.uk/news/media/martin-glenn-mr-can-do-307503.html.

23. "Walkers Launches into Low-Fat Crisps Market," *MarketingWeek*, Oct. 11, 1996, https://www.marketingweek.com/walkers-launches-into-low-fat-crisps-market/.

24. Joe Lepper, "Walkers to Launch Healthier Potato Heads Crisp Range," Campaignlive.com, Oct. 25, 2004, https://www.campaignlive.com/article/walkers-launch-healthier-potato-heads-crisp-range/225925.

25. "Martin Glenn: Mr Can Do."

26. "Martin Glenn: Mr Can Do."

27. "Martin Glenn: Walkers' First Mr Nice Guy," Campaignlive.co.uk, June 3, 2005, https://www.campaignlive.co.uk/article/martin-glenn -walkers-first-mr-nice-guy/478612.

28. "Martin Glenn: Walkers' First Mr Nice Guy."

29. Sandile Zungu and John Dludlu, "Maseko Leaves Behind a Success Story at Telkom as Outgoing Chief Executive," Sowetan Live, Aug. 31, 2021, https://www.sowetanlive.co.za/opinion/columnists /2021-08-31-maseko-leaves-behind-a-success-story-at-telkom-as -outgoing-chief-executive/.

30. "Modernizing America's Transmission Network," Environmental and Energy Study Institute, June 11, 2021, https://www.eesi.org /briefings/view/061121grid.

31. Anita Elberse, "Ferguson's Formula," *Harvard Business Review*," October 2013, https://hbr.org/2013/10/fergusons-formula.

32. Ryan Bailey, "David Beckham Describes the Day He Signed for Manchester United," BleacherReport.com, Oct. 15, 2013, https:// bleacherreport.com/articles/2579468-david-beckham-describes-the -day-he-signed-for-manchester-united.

33. Sam Pilger, "David Beckham Enjoyed His Best Years at Manchester United," BleacherReport.com, May 16, 2013, https://bleacherreport .com/articles/1641866-david-beckham-enjoyed-his-best-years-at -manchester-united.

34. Elberse, "Ferguson's Formula."

35. "Ryan Giggs Biography," Manchester United, https://www.manutd .com/en/players-and-staff/detail/ryan-giggs.

36. Elberse, "Ferguson's Formula."

37. Elberse, "Ferguson's Formula."

38. Elberse, "Ferguson's Formula."

39. Elberse, "Ferguson's Formula."

40. Adam Crafton et al., "What Made Sir Alex Ferguson So Successful?" Dec. 25, 2021, *The Athletic*, https://theathletic.com/3033467 /2021/12/26/manchester-united-what-made-sir-alex-ferguson-so -successful/.

41. Crafton et al., "What Made Sir Alex Ferguson So Successful?"

42. Crafton et al., "What Made Sir Alex Ferguson So Successful?"

## CHAPTER 5

1. "Executive Team: Howard Schultz," Starbucks, https://stories .starbucks.com/leadership/howard-schultz/.

2. Julia Hanna, "Starbucks, Reinvented: A Seven-Year Study On Schultz, Strategy And Reinventing A Brilliant Brand," Forbes.com, August 25, 2014, https://www.forbes.com /sites/hbsworkingknowledge/2014/08/25/starbucks-reinvented/?sh= 35698c3930d0.

3. Mikaela Parrick, "11 Corporate Turnaround Success Stories," Brownandjoseph.com, March 6, 2018, https://brownandjoseph.com /blog/11-turnaround-success-stories/.

4. Shezray Husain, Feroz Khan, and Waqas Mirza, "How Starbucks pulled itself out of the 2008 financial meltdown," businesstoday.in, September 28, 2014, https://www.businesstoday.in/magazine/lbs -case-study/story/how-starbucks-survived-the-financial-meltdown -of-2008-136126-2014-09-22.

5. "Starbucks, Reinvented: A Seven-Year Study On Schultz, Strategy And Reinventing A Brilliant Brand."

6. "Starbucks, Reinvented: A Seven-Year Study On Schultz, Strategy And Reinventing A Brilliant Brand."

7. Howard Schultz with Joanne Gordon, *Onward: How Starbucks Fought for Its Life without Losing Its Soul* (Rodale, 2011).

8. "Financial Data," Starbucks, https://investor.starbucks.com /financial-data/annual-reports/default.aspx.

9. "A Message from Larry Merlo," CVSHealth.com, April 2, 2021, https://cvshealth2020inreview.com/larry-merlo-message.

10. "A Message from Larry Merlo."

11. "Our Purpose," CVS Health,' https://www.cvshealth.com/about-cvs -health/our-purpose.

12. Felicity Lawrence, "How Food Producers Were Forced to Change Their Tastes," *The Guardian*, April 25, 2006, https://www .theguardian.com/society/2006/apr/25/health.lifeandhealth.

13. Lawrence, "How Food Producers Were Forced to Change Their Tastes."

14. Lawrence, "How Food Producers Were Forced to Change Their Tastes."

15. Lawrence, "How Food Producers Were Forced to Change Their Tastes."

16. Satya Nadella with Greg Shaw and Jill Tracie Nichols, *Hit Refresh: The Quest to Rediscover Microsoft's Soul and Imagine a Better Future for Everyone* (Harper Business, updated edition, 2017), Kindle.

17. Cara Lombardo, Kirsten Grind, and Aaron Tilley, "Microsoft to Buy Activision Blizzard in All-Cash Deal Valued at $75 Billion," *Wall Street Journal*, Jan. 18, 2022, https://www.wsj.com/articles/microsoft-to-buy-activision-blizzard-games-11642512435?mod=hp_lead_pos1.

18. Lombardo, Grind, and Tilley, "Microsoft to Buy Activision Blizzard."

19. Karen Weise et al., "Microsoft Will Buy Activision Blizzard, Betting $70 Billion on the Future of Games," *New York Times*, Jan. 18, 2022, https://www.nytimes.com/2022/01/18/business/microsoft-activision-blizzard.html.

20. "Microsoft CEO Satya Nadella Just Laid Out the Company's Vision for Its 'Netflix for Games,'" Business Insider, Jan. 16, 2019, https://www.businessinsider.com/microsoft-ceo-satya-nadella-xbox-netflix-for-games-2019-1.

21. Harrison Abbott, "Why Has Microsoft Bought Activision Blizzard and How Much is the Deal Worth?" *Newsweek*, Jan. 18, 2022, https://www.newsweek.com/microsoft-activision-blizzard-deal-how-much-acquisition-1670324.

22. "Microsoft to Acquire Activision Blizzard to Bring the Joy and Community of Gaming to Everyone, Across Every Device," Microsoft.com, Jan. 18, 2022, https://news.microsoft.com/features/microsoft-to-acquire-activision-blizzard-to-bring-the-joy-and-community-of-gaming-to-everyone-across-every-device/.

23. Satya Nadella, Bobby Kotick, Amy Hood, and Phil Spencer, "Microsoft and Activision Blizzard Investor Call," Microsoft.com, Jan. 18, 2022, https://www.microsoft.com/en-us/Investor/events/FY-2022/Microsoft-and-Activision-Blizzard-Conference-Call.

## CHAPTER 6

1. "Edwin Hubble," NASA, https://www.nasa.gov/content/about-story-edwin-hubble.

2. "Edwin Hubble," NASA.

3. "Edwin Hubble Changed Our Ideas About the Universe and Its Birth," Voice of America—Europe, Oct. 31, 2012, https://learningenglish.voanews.com/a/edwin-hubble-changed-our-ideas-about-the-universe-and-its-birth/1537071.html.

4. "Edwin Hubble Changed Our Ideas."

5. "Edwin Hubble: The Man Who Discovered the Cosmos," European Space Agency, Dec. 8, 2012, https://www.esa.int/About_Us/ESA_history/Edwin_Hubble_The_man_who_discovered_the_Cosmos.

6. "Edwin Hubble," NASA; "Edwin Hubble Changed Our Ideas."

7. Brandon Gage, "95 Years Ago, Edwin Hubble Changed the World," Chosen Magazine, Oct. 7, 2018, http://www.chosenmag.com/95-years-ago-edwin-hubble-changed-the-world/2018/10/7/95-years-ago-edwin-hubble-changed-the-world.

8. "Edwin Hubble," NASA.

9. Stephanie Pappas, "The Day Edwin Hubble Realized Our Universe Was Expanding, LiveScience.com, Jan. 17, 2019, https://www.livescience.com/64527-edwin-hubble-universe-expanding.html.

10. Deborah Byrd, "Edwin Hubble and the Expanding Universe," EarthSky, Nov. 20, 2021, https://earthsky.org/space/this-date-in-science-edwin-hubble-and-the-expanding-universe/.

11. "People and Discoveries: Edwin Hubble," PBS.org, https://www.pbs.org/wgbh/aso/databank/entries/bahubb.html.

12. "Edwin Hubble," NASA.

13. "Edwin Hubble Changed Our Ideas."

14. "Edwin Hubble: The Man Who Discovered the Cosmos."

15. "Case Files: Edwin Hubble," The Franklin Institute, https://www.fi.edu/case-files/edwin-hubble.

16. "People and Discoveries: Henrietta Leavitt," PBS.org, https://www.pbs.org/wgbh/aso/databank/entries/baleav.html.

17. Leila McNeill, "The 'Star-Fiend' Who Unlocked the Universe," BBC, March 11, 2021, https://www.bbc.com/future/article/20210310-the-star-fiend-who-unlocked-the-universe.

18. "10 Warren Bennis Quotes on Leadership in Business," iU eMagazine, June 3, 2017, https://www.iuemag.com/u17/di/10-warren-bennis-quotes-on-leadership-in-business.php.

19. "How Long Does It Take to Train for a Marathon?" ASICS, https://www.asics.com/gb/en-gb/running-advice/how-long-does-it-take-to-train-for-a-marathon/.

20. Satya Nadella with Greg Shaw and Jill Tracie Nichols, *Hit Refresh: The Quest to Rediscover Microsoft's Soul and Imagine a Better Future for Everyone* (Harper Business, updated edition, 2017), Kindle.

21. Steven Handel, "10 Lessons in Zen Leadership Practiced by Legendary Coach Phil Jackson," The Emotion Machine, https://www.theemotionmachine.com/10-lessons-in-zen-leadership-practiced-by-legendary-coach-phil-jackson/.

22. Donnovan Bennett, "23 from No. 23: The Best Quotes from 'The Last Dance,'" Sportsnet.ca, May 18, 2020, https://www.sportsnet.ca/basketball/nba/23-no-23-best-quotes-last-dance/.

23. Jason Hehir, dir., *The Last Dance* (miniseries), 2020, ESPN Films and Netflix; clip on Facebook post, Daniel Sigrist, Aug. 11, 2020, https://www.facebook.com/100063829883613/videos/693402774584867/.

24. Carmine Gallo, "How Steve Jobs and Bill Gates Inspired John Sculley to Pursue the 'Noble Cause,'" Forbes.com, Nov. 12, 2016, https://www.forbes.com/sites/carminegallo/2016/11/12/how-steve-jobs-and-bill-gates-inspired-john-sculley-to-pursue-the-noble-cause/.

25. "Larry J. Merlo, President and Chief Executive Officer, CVS Health," CVSHealth.com, February, 2019, https://s2.q4cdn.com/447711729/files/doc_events/2019/InvestorDay2019/02-Exec-Bios.pdf.

26. "Success Is Not Final; Failure Is Not Fatal: It Is the Courage to Continue That Counts." –Winston Churchill," Business Standard, April 23, 2021, https://www.business-standard.com/content/specials/success-is-not-final-failure-is-not-fatal-it-is-the-courage-to-continue-that-counts-winston-churchill-121042300664_1.html.

27. Joel Siegel, "When Steve Jobs Got Fired by Apple," ABCNews.com, Oct. 6, 2011, https://abcnews.go.com/Technology/steve-jobs-fire-company/story?id=14683754.

28. "Our Story," Pixar, https://www.pixar.com/our-story-pixar#:~:text=1986,about%2040%20people%20are%20employed.

29. "Steve Jobs Quotes," BrainyQuote.com, https://www.brainyquote.com/quotes/steve_jobs_416857.

30. "Robert Allen Quotes," Goodreads.com, https://www.goodreads.com/quotes/9597909-there-is-no-failure-only-feedback.

31. Jim Collins, "The Stockdale Paradox, " JimCollins.com, https://www.jimcollins.com/concepts/Stockdale-Concept.html.

32. Noor Zainab Hussain and Joshua Franklin, "Airbnb Valuation Surges Past $100 Billion in Biggest U.S. IPO of 2020," Reuters .com, Dec. 2020, https://www.reuters.com/article/airbnb-ipo /airbnb-valuation-surges-past-100-billion-in-biggest-u-s-ipo-of -2020-idUSKBN28K261.

33. "Martin Glenn: Football Must Work Together to Put Fans First," The FA, May 19, 2015, https://www.thefa.com/news/2015/may/19 /martin-glenn-first-interview.

34. "Martin Glenn: Football Must Work Together."

35. Jack Zenger and Joseph Folkman, "What Great Listeners Actually Do," *Harvard Business Review*, July 14, 2016, https://hbr.org/2016 /07/what-great-listeners-actually-do.

36. Jason Aten, "Disney's Former CEO Bob Iger Just Explained Why He Resigned," *Inc.*, https://www.inc.com/jason-aten/disneys-former -ceo-bob-iger-just-explained-reason-he-resigned-its-best-example -of-emotional-intelligence-ive-seen-yet.html.

37. *The 4-Hour Body*, FourHourBody.com, https://fourhourbody.com /contents/.

38. Jerry Rice, https://www.jerryricefootball.com/about.

39. Roberta Naas, "Tom Brady Talks About Time, Hard Work and Success," *Forbes*, July 9, 2020, https://www.forbes.com/sites/robertanaas /2020/07/09/tom-brady-talks-about-time-hard-work-success-iwc -watches/?sh=55e41ba79aa9.

40. "Tom Brady on the Early-Career Struggles That Forged His Superstardom," BestLife, May 9, 2017, https://bestlifeonline.com/tom -brady-defining-moment/.

41. "Saad Abdul-Latif, PepsiCo CEO for AMEA Region, Dies," Mint, Aug. 20, 2013, https://www.livemint.com/Companies /t7f8GDACLLhKRsAdfVYDgK/Saad-AbdulLatif-PepsiCo -CEO-for-AMEA-region-dies.html.

42. Ray Dalio, "Principle of the Day," LinkedIn.com, February 2019, https://www.linkedin.com/posts/raydalio_there-is-no-avoiding -pain-especially-if-activity-6592757368541466624-NqMW/.

43. "Ray Dalio's Son's Death Ruled Accident Caused by Smoke Inhalation, Burns Following Fiery Crash: Officials," FoxNews.com, Jan. 25, 2021, https://www.foxnews.com/us/devon-dalio-ray-dalio -accident-greenwich-connecticut.

44. Ray Dalio, "My Reflections Six Weeks After My Son's Passing," LinkedIn, Feb. 10, 2021, https://www.linkedin.com/pulse/my -reflections-six-weeks-after-sons-passing-ray-dalio/.

**CHAPTER 7**

1. Sarah Jackson, "Elizabeth Holmes Is Dealt a Blow as the Judge in Her Fraud Case Tentatively Denied Her Request to Throw Out Her Conviction," Business Insider, Sept. 2, 2022, https://www .businessinsider.com/elizabeth-holmes-theranos-judge-denies-her -request-to-toss-conviction-2022-9.
2. "Hot Startup Theranos Has Struggled With Its Blood-Test Technology," *Wall Street Journal*, Oct. 16, 2015, https://www.wsj.com /articles/theranos-has-struggled-with-blood-tests-1444881901?mod =article_inline.
3. Taylor Dunn, Victoria Thompson, and Rebecca Jarvis, "Ex-Theranos Employees Describe Culture of Secrecy at Elizabeth Holmes Startup," ABC News, March 12, 2019, https://abcnews.go.com /Business/theranos-employees-describe-culture-secrecy-elizabeth -holmes-startup/story?id=60544673.
4. Sara Randazzo, "A Theranos Timeline: The Downfall of Elizabeth Holmes, a Silicon Valley Superstar," *Wall Street Journal*, Sept. 13, 2021, https://www.wsj.com/articles/a-theranos-timeline -the-downfall-of-elizabeth-holmes-a-silicon-valley-superstar -11631576110.
5. Stephen Jones, "What Theranos Can Teach You About Silos," *Management Today*, Sept. 4, 2020, https://www.managementtoday.co.uk /theranos-teach-silos/food-for-thought/article/1693529.
6. Alicia Geigel, "Everything to Know About *Bad Blood*, the New Theranos Movie Starring Jennifer Lawrence," PopSugar, Dec. 17, 2021, https://www.yahoo.com/now/everything-know-bad-blood -theranos-002131460.html.
7. Tom Relihan, "4 Red Flags That Signaled Theranos' Downfall," MIT Sloan School of Management, Oct. 29, 2018, https://mitsloan .mit.edu/ideas-made-to-matter/4-red-flags-signaled-theranos -downfall.
8. Nick Bilton, "'She Never Looks Back': Inside Elizabeth Holmes's Chilling Final Months at Theranos," *Vanity Fair*, Feb. 20, 2019,

https://www.vanityfair.com/news/2019/02/inside-elizabeth
-holmess-final-months-at-theranos.

9. "Theranos, CEO Holmes, and Former President Balwani Charged with Massive Fraud," U.S. Securities and Exchange Commission, March 14, 2018, https://www.sec.gov/news/press-release/2018-41.

10. "Theranos Founder Elizabeth Holmes Found Guilty of Investor Fraud," U.S. Attorney's Office Northern District of California, U.S. Department of Justice, Jan. 4, 2022, https://www.justice.gov/usao -ndca/pr/theranos-founder-elizabeth-holmes-found-guilty-investor -fraud.

11. Wills Robinson, "Award-Winning Scientist Who Was Struggling to Make Theranos Blood Test Machines Work Committed Suicide Amid Fears Silicon Valley Firm's 32-Year Old CEO Was About to Fire Him, Claims Wife," *Daily Mail*, Sept. 7, 2016, https://www .dailymail.co.uk/news/article-3776888/Award-winning-scientist -struggling-make-Theranos-blood-test-machines-work-committed -suicide-amid-fears-Silicon-Valley-firm-s-32-year-old-CEO-fire -claims-wife.html.

12. Monica Torres, "4 Ways Elizabeth Holmes Manipulated Her Theranos Employees," HuffPost, March 22, 2019, updated Nov. 18, 2022, https://www.huffpost.com/entry/elizabeth-holmes-office-employee s_l_5c92abe3e4b01b140d351b6f.

13. Larry Senn, "Four Key Reasons Culture Change Initiatives Fail," Themoodelevator.com, July 15, 2017, https://themoodelevator.com /corporate-culture/four-key-reasons-culture-change-initiatives-fail/.

14. Brian Kachejian, "The History of Woolworths," ClassicNew YorkHistory.com, 2022, https://classicnewyorkhistory.com/the -history-of-woolworths/; Brian O'Connell, "History of Walmart: Timeline and Facts," TheStreet, Jan. 2, 2020, https://www .thestreet.com/markets/history-of-walmart-15092339.

15. "'Transformation Needs Transparency and a Clear Vision': Wendy Clark, CEO of Dentsu International," n.d., https://www.pwc.co.uk /ceo-survey/insights/transparency-in-business-transformation-to -succeed.html.

16. "Transformation Needs Transparency and a Clear Vision."

17. Gideon Spanier, "Dentsu's Wendy Clark: 'If I Don't Use My Position to Change the Face of the Industry, Shame on Me,'" Campaign

US, Feb. 18, 2021, https://www.campaignlive.com/article/dentsus-wendy-clark-if-i-dont-use-position-change-face-industry-shame-me/1707732.

18. Spanier, "Dentsu's Wendy Clark."

19. Ed Manfre and Dustin Seale, "Culture Comes First: What Separates Slow-Growth Companies from 'Culture Accelerators,'" LinkedIn.com, July 22, 2021, https://www.linkedin.com/pulse/culture-comes-first-what-separates-slow-growth-companies-ed-manfre/.

20. Claire Duffy, "How Bob Iger Celebrated His Last Day at Disney After Nearly 50 Years," CNN.com, Dec. 31, 2021, https://www.cnn.com/2021/12/31/media/bob-iger-exits-disney/index.html.

21. Matt Krantz, "Was Bob Iger the Best Disney CEO Ever for Investors?" Investors.com, Feb. 26, 2020, https://www.investors.com/etfs-and-funds/personal-finance/bob-iger-vs-michael-eisner-who-was-best-disney-ceo/.

22. Meg James, "How Disney's Bob Iger Went from Underrated CEO to Hollywood Royalty," *Los Angeles Times*, March 1, 2020, https://www.latimes.com/entertainment-arts/business/story/2020-03-01/bob-iger-transformed-disney-and-hollywood.

23. James, "How Disney's Bob Iger Went from Underrated CEO to Hollywood Royalty."

24. Lacey Rose, "Disney's Bob Iger Talks Steve Jobs, Lucasfilm and His Biggest Fear," *Hollywood Reporter*, Jan. 23, 2013, https://www.hollywoodreporter.com/news/general-news/disneys-bob-iger-steve-jobs-414954/.

25. Cory Stieg, "How Bob Iger Convinced Steve Jobs to Sell Pixar to Disney: 'I've Got a Crazy Idea,'" CNBC, Dec. 2, 2020, https://www.cnbc.com/2020/12/02/bob-iger-on-how-he-convinced-steve-jobs-to-sell-pixar-to-disney.html.

26. Swapnil Dhruv Bose, "How Bob Iger Changed Disney: 15 Years of the Disney-Pixar Merger," *Far Out*, March 2021, https://faroutmagazine.co.uk/how-bob-iger-changed-disney-pixar-merger/.

27. Stieg, "How Bob Iger Convinced Steve Jobs to Sell Pixar"; "What Steve Jobs Told Bob Iger Just Before Disney Bought Pixar," Bloomberg.com, Dec. 2, 2020, https://www.bloomberg.com/news/videos/2020-12-02/what-steve-jobs-told-bob-iger-just-before-disney-bought-pixar-video.

28. Stieg, "How Bob Iger Convinced Steve Jobs to Sell Pixar."

29. Laura M. Holson, "Disney Agrees to Acquire Pixar in a $7.4 Billion Deal," *New York Times*, Jan. 26, 2006, https://www.nytimes.com/2006/01/25/business/disney-agrees-to-acquire-pixar-in-a-74-billion-deal.html.

30. Jade Scipioni, "10 Principles for Great Leadership, According to Disney's Bob Iger," CNBC.com, Oct. 23, 2019, https://www.cnbc.com/2019/10/23/disney-ceo-bob-igers-principles-for-great-leadership.html.

31. Carmine Gallo, "In a New MasterClass, Bob Iger Reveals the Communication Tactic He Used to Land the Job as Disney CEO," Inc.com, Nov. 20, 2019, https://www.inc.com/carmine-gallo/in-a-new-masterclass-bob-iger-reveals-communication-tactic-he-used-to-land-job-as-disney-ceo.html.

32. Rosa Braceras, "Get to Know Alex Cora: Stats, Managerial Career and More," NBCSports.com, Aug. 16, 2022, https://www.nbcsports.com/boston/red-sox/alex-cora.

33. Richard Tovar, "Houston Astros in MLB World Series: Championships and Appearances," BolaVIP.com, Oct. 27, 2021, https://bolavip.com/en/mlb/houston-astros-in-mlb-world-series-championships-and-appearances-20211027-0007.html.

34. Tyler Kepner, "Red Sox' Alex Cora Suspended Through 2020 in Sign-Stealing Scandal," *New York Times*, April 22, 2020, https://www.nytimes.com/2020/04/22/sports/baseball/alex-cora-red-sox-sign-stealing.html.

35. Kelly Cohen, "MLB Playoffs 2021: Houston Astros Timeline from Sign-Stealing Scandal to Another World Series," ESPN.com, Oct. 23, 2021, https://www.espn.com/mlb/story/_/id/32452834/mlb-playoffs-2021-houston-astros-line-sign-stealing-scandal-another-world-series.

36. "The Houston Astros' Cheating Scandal: Sign-Stealing, Buzzer Intrigue and Tainted Pennants," *New York Times*, Nov. 3, 2021, https://www.nytimes.com/article/astros-cheating.html.

37. Chad Jennings, "How Alex Cora and the Red Sox Reunited: 'It Wasn't a Dog-and-Pony Show,'" *The Athletic*, Nov. 5, 2020, https://theathletic.com/2183812/2020/11/06/alex-cora-chaim-bloom-red-sox/.

38. Chad Jennings, "The Red Sox Just Ran Through a Wall for Alex Cora. Or Maybe It Just Felt like They Did," *The Athletic*, Oct. 12, 2021, https://theathletic.com/2883853/2021/10/12/the-red-sox-just-ran-through-a-wall-for-alex-cora-or-maybe-it-just-felt-like-they-did/.

39. Jennings, "The Red Sox Just Ran Through a Wall for Alex Cora."

40. Jennings, "The Red Sox Just Ran Through a Wall for Alex Cora."

41. Bob Hohler, "After a Humbling Suspension, Alex Cora's Resilience Was Evident as He Nearly Made History with Red Sox," *Boston Globe*, Oct. 28, 2021, https://www.bostonglobe.com/2021/10/28/sports/alex-cora-red-sox-2021-season/.

42. Ty Anderson, "Red Sox Manager Alex Cora Gives Emotional Interview Following ALDS-Clinching Win," 98.5 The Sports Hub, Oct. 12, 2021, https://985thesportshub.com/2021/10/12/red-sox-manager-alex-cora-gives-emotional-interview-following-alds-clinching-win/.

43. Ray Dalio, *Principles: Life and Work* (New York: Simon & Schuster, 2017).

## CHAPTER 8

1. Laura O'Callaghan, "How Flyers Fell Out of Love with British Airways," The National, April 8, 2022, https://www.thenationalnews.com/weekend/2022/04/08/how-flyers-fell-out-of-love-with-british-airways/.

2. "Explore Our Past," BritishAirways.com, https://www.britishairways.com/en-us/information/about-ba/history-and-heritage/explore-our-past.

3. "Even More Cheap Flights to Europe Coming in 2018," TravelSkills.com, Nov. 28, 2017, https://travelskills.com/tag/british-airways/.

4. Eshe Nelson, "British Airways Abruptly Replaces Its Chief Executive," *New York Times*, Oct. 12, 2020, https://www.nytimes.com/2020/10/12/business/british-airways-ceo.html.

5. Esther Marshall, "British Airways Vows to Bring Back BA 'Golden Age' with New Rules—but No Free G&T," Express, Nov. 21, 2021, https://www.express.co.uk/travel/articles/1518728/british-airways-ba-baggage-allowance-seat-room-refreshment.

6. Gabriel Power, "Why British Airways Has Nosedived with Passengers," The Week, Dec. 19, 2019, https://www.theweek.co.uk/104957/why-british-airways-has-nosedived-with-passengers.

7. Terry Nguyen, "A Brief History of Airline Worker Strikes," Vox.com, Sept. 11, 2019, https://www.vox.com/the-goods/2019/9/11/20860891/british-airways-history-worker-strikes.

8. Graeme Paton, "BA Settles Pilots Dispute and Averts Threat of More Strikes," Times, Dec. 17, 2019, https://www.thetimes.co.uk/article/ba-settles-pilots-dispute-and-averts-threat-of-more-strikes-shj5nr98w.

9. Theo Leggett, "British Airways: A Breakdown in Trust?" BBC.com, June 12, 2020, https://www.bbc.com/news/business-53023563.

10. Betsy Reed, "Álex Cruz Steps Down as BA Chief After Covid Job Cuts Row," The Guardian, Oct. 12, 2020, https://www.theguardian.com/business/2020/oct/12/alex-cruz-ba-covid-job-cuts-british-airways-sean-doyle.

11. Philip Georgiadis, "BA Boss Pledges to Rebuild Its Reputation for Premium Service," Financial Times, Jan. 28, 2022, https://www.ft.com/content/473f9eee-6e8e-49fb-a020-1da305ff4430.

12. Georgiadis, "BA Boss Pledges to Rebuild Its Reputation for Premium Service."

13. Marshall, "British Airways Vows to Bring Back BA 'Golden Age.'"

14. Matt Lennon, "British Airways Sets Flight Path Back to Being a Premium Airline," Executive Traveller, Feb. 4, 2022, https://www.executivetraveller.com/news/british-airways-ceo-sets-flight-path-back-to-being-a-premium-airline.

15. "What Is ESG (Environmental, Social and Governance)?" Diligent.com, https://www.diligent.com/insights/esg/.

16. "2022 Edelman Trust Barometer," Edelman, January 31, 2022, https://www.edelman.de/en/research/edelman-trust-barometer-2022.

17. Paul J. Zak, "The Neuroscience of Trust," Harvard Business Review, January-February 2017, https://hbr.org/2017/01/the-neuroscience-of-trust.

18. Rose Gailey, Ian Johnston, and Andrew LeSueur, "Aligning Culture with the Bottom Line: How Companies Can Accelerate Progress,"

2021, Heidrick.com, https://www.heidrick.com/en/insights/culture -shaping/aligning-culture-with-the-bottom-line-how-companies -can-accelerate-progress.

19. "Our Purpose," CVSHealth, https://www.cvshealth.com/about-cvs -health/our-purpose.

20. "Nelson Henderson Quotes and Sayings," InspiringQuotes.US, https://www.inspiringquotes.us/author/9941-nelson-henderson.

21. Nathan Bomey, "How Quitting Tobacco Reshaped CVS: Q&A with Larry Merlo," *USA Today*, Sept. 4, 2019, https://www.usatoday .com/story/money/2019/09/03/cvs-pharmacy-tobacco-sales-ceo -larry-merlo/2151148001/.

22. "After CVS Stopped Cigarette Sales, Smokers Stopped Buying Else-where, Too," *Forbes*, Feb. 20, 2017, https://www.forbes.com/sites /brucejapsen/2017/02/20/after-cvs-stopped-cigarette-sales-smokers -stopped-buying-elsewhere-too/.

23. Alicia Adamczyk, "Say Goodbye to 9-to-5: More and More, Cor-porate America Is Letting People Work Whenever They Want," *Fortune*, March 21, 2022.

## CHAPTER 9

1. Robin Wigglesworth, "The Ten Trillion Dollar Man: How Larry Fink Became King of Wall St," *Financial Times*, Oct. 6, 2021, https:// www.ft.com/content/7dfd1e3d-e256-4656-a96d-1204538d75cd.

2. Ganesha Cherukuthota, "Laurence D. Fink: The Leader Who Shaped Today's Investment Management Landscape," The Financial Pandora, Jan. 28, 2021, https://thefinancialpandora.com/laurence -d-fink/.

3. "The Bond Market: A Look Back," Investopedia.com, June 11, 2021, updated August 9, 2022, https://www.investopedia.com/articles/06 /centuryofbonds.asp.

4. Wigglesworth, "The Ten Trillion Dollar Man."

5. Suzanna Andrews, "Larry Fink's $12 Trillion Shadow," *Vanity Fair*, April 2010, https://www.vanityfair.com/news/2010/04/fink -201004.

6. Cherukuthota, "Laurence D. Fink"; Global Structured Finance 2022 Outlook," S&P Global, Jan. 12, 2022, https://www.spglobal .com/_assets/documents/ratings/research/100993747.pdf.

7. Cherukuthota, "Laurence D. Fink."

8. Andrews, "Larry Fink's $12 Trillion Shadow."

9. Wigglesworth, "The Ten Trillion Dollar Man."

10. Wigglesworth, "The Ten Trillion Dollar Man."

11. Andrews, "Larry Fink's $12 Trillion Shadow."

12. Andrews, "Larry Fink's $12 Trillion Shadow."

13. Andrews, "Larry Fink's $12 Trillion Shadow."

14. "Ideas, Innovations and Growth," BlackRock, March 31, 2020, https://www.blackrock.com/corporate/about-us/blackrock-history.

15. Rebecca Ungarino, "Here Are 9 Fascinating Facts to Know About BlackRock, the World's Largest Asset Manager," Business Insider, March 10, 2022, https://www.businessinsider.com/what-to-know-about-blackrock-larry-fink-biden-cabinet-facts-2020-12.

16. Annie Massa, "BlackRock Boosts Fink's Pay 21% to $36 Million for Last Year," Bloomberg, April 14, 2022, https://www.bloomberg.com/news/articles/2022-04-14/blackrock-boosts-fink-s-pay-21-to-36-million-for-last-year.

17. "Larry Fink, Cofounder, CEO, BlackRock," *Forbes*, April 4, 2022, https://www.forbes.com/profile/larry-fink/?sh=6c50045c20f4.

18. Andrews, "Larry Fink's $12 Trillion Shadow."

19. "Larry Fink's 2012 Letter to CEOs," BlackRock, 2012, https://www.blackrock.com/corporate/investor-relations/2012-larry-fink-ceo-letter.

20. "Larry Fink's 2014 Letter to CEOs."

21. "A Fundamental Reshaping of Finance: Larry Fink's 2020 Letter to CEOs," BlackRock, 2020, https://www.blackrock.com/us/individual/larry-fink-ceo-letter.

22. "Larry Fink's 2021 Letter to CEOs," BlackRock, 2021, https://www.blackrock.com/corporate/investor-relations/2021-larry-fink-ceo-letter.

23. "The Power of Capitalism: Larry Fink's 2022 Letter to CEOs," BlackRock, 2022, https://www.blackrock.com/corporate/investor-relations/larry-fink-ceo-letter.

24. "The Power of Capitalism: Larry Fink's 2022 Letter to CEOs."

25. "2022 Edelman Trust Barometer," Edelman, Jan. 18, 2022, https://www.edelman.com/trust/2022-trust-barometer.

26. "The Complexities of Trust: PwC's Trust in US Business Survey," PricewaterhouseCoopers, 2022, https://www.pwc.com/us/en/library/trust-in-business-survey.html.

27. Tim Ryan, "How Business Can Build and Maintain Trust," *Harvard Business Review*, Feb. 7, 2022, https://hbr.org/2022/02/how-business-can-build-and-maintain-trust.

28. "The Complexities of Trust."

29. Ryan, "How Business Can Build and Maintain Trust."

30. Ed Manfre, "Leadership in This Era Is a Matter of Trust. But What Does That Mean?" LinkedIn.com, April 5, 2022, https://www.linkedin.com/pulse/leadership-era-matter-trust-what-does-mean-ed-manfre/.

31. "A Conversation with General Robles," Oliver Wyman, October 2015, https://www.oliverwyman.com/content/dam/oliver-wyman/global/en/2015/oct/Conversation_With_General_Robles.pdf.

32. "A Conversation with General Robles."

33. "A Conversation with General Robles."

34. "USAA Increases Minimum Pay to $21 per Hour for All Employees," USAA, Oct. 11, 2021, https://communities.usaa.com/t5/Press-Releases/USAA-Increases-Minimum-Pay-to-21-per-Hour-for-All-Employees/ba-p/253057.

35. "Joe Robles," LinkedIn.com, 2022, https://www.linkedin.com/in/joe-robles-20252148/.

36. "USAA CEO Joe Robles Reveals Why Culture Has Given the Company a Huge Competitive Edge in a New Thought Leadership Video by Culture Shaping Firm Senn Delaney," PRWeb.com, Oct. 9, 2012, https://www.prweb.com/releases/2012senndelaneyceovideos/usaaceojoerobles/prweb9991117.htm.

37. "Our Mission," Axios.

38. "What Exactly Is a 'News Desert'?" Center for Innovation and Sustainability in Local Media, Hussman School of Journalism and Media, University of North Carolina, https://www.cislm.org/what-exactly-is-a-news-desert/.

39. Brier Dudley, "New Report Finds U.S. 'News Desert' Spreading, More Papers Closing," *Seattle Times*, July 1, 2022, https://www.seattletimes.com/opinion/new-report-finds-u-s-news-desert-spreading-more-papers-closing/.

40. Erin Karter, "As Newspapers Close, Struggling Communities Are Hit Hardest by the Decline in Local Journalism," Northwestern Now, June 29, 2022, https://news.northwestern.edu/stories/2022/06/newspapers-close-decline-in-local-journalism/.

41. Karter, "As Newspapers Close."

42. André Tassinari, "4 Media Ventures That Failed," *Columbia Journalism Review*, May 11, 2015, https://www.cjr.org/the_experiment/4_media_ventures_that_failed.php.

43. Jim VandeHei, "The Rise of Aspirational Capitalism," Axios, May 26, 2022, https://www.axios.com/2022/05/27/aspirational-capitalism-business-trend.

44. VandeHei, "The Rise of Aspirational Capitalism."

45. Luke Daniel, "Meet Telkom's New CEO Serame Taukobong—the Man Who Revived Its Mobile Business," Business Insider South Africa, Aug. 5, 2021, https://www.businessinsider.co.za/who-is-serame-taukobong-new-telkom-ceo-2021-8.

46. Admire Moyo, "Market Lauds Telkom as Maseko Hands Baton to Taukobong," ITWeb, Aug. 5, 2021, https://www.itweb.co.za/content/rxP3jMBmoEP7A2ye.

47. "Telkom CEO Sipho Maseko Leaves Six Months Early," MyBroadband, Dec. 14, 2021, https://mybroadband.co.za/news/telecoms/427480-telkom-ceo-sipho-maseko-leaves-six-months-early.html.

## CONCLUSION

1. "The War in 1863," Britannica, https://www.britannica.com/event/American-Civil-War/The-war-in-the-east.

2. "Troops in the Campaign, Siege, and Defense of Vicksburg," National Park Service, https://www.nps.gov/vick/learn/historyculture/copy-of-troops-in-the-campaign-siege-and-defense-of-vicksburg.htm.

3. "The War in 1863."

4. "The Lincoln Family," U.S. National Park Service, https://www.nps.gov/liho/learn/historyculture/the-lincoln-family.htm.

5. Amy S. Greenberg, "Pulling Back the Curtain on the Lincoln's Marriage," review of *An American Marriage: The Untold Story of Abraham Lincoln and Mary Todd*, by Michael Burlingame, *New York Times*, June 7, 2021, Book Review, https://www.nytimes.com/2021/06/01/books/review/michael-burlingame-an-american-marriage-abraham-lincoln-mary-todd.html.

6. "Appomattox Court House: Lee's Surrender," American Battle-field Trust, https://www.battlefields.org/learn/civil-war/battles/appomattox-court-house.

7. "The Lincoln Family."

8. Bob Zeller, "How Many Died in the American Civil War?" History.com, Jan. 6, 2022, https://www.history.com/news/american-civil-war-deaths.

9. "Abraham Lincoln, 1809–1865," *Smithsonian*, https://www.si.edu/spotlight/highlights-abraham-lincoln-1809-1865.

10. "WHO Coronavirus (Covid-19) Dashboard," World Health Organization, June 14, 2022, https://covid19.who.int; Gwynn Guilford, "U.S. Inflation Hits 8.6% in May, *Wall Street Journal*, June 10, 2022, https://www.wsj.com/articles/us-inflation-consumer-price-index-may-2022-11654810079.

11. Ashley Abramson, "Burnout and Stress Are Everywhere: 2022 Trends Survey," American Psychological Association, Jan. 1, 2022, https://www.apa.org/monitor/2022/01/special-burnout-stress.

12. "Burn-Out an 'Occupational Phenomenon': International Classification of Diseases," World Health Organization, May 28, 2019, https://www.who.int/news/item/28-05-2019-burn-out-an-occupational-phenomenon-international-classification-of-diseases.

# INDEX

Page numbers followed by *f* refer to figures.

# ABOUT THE AUTHORS

**Dustin Seale** has been advising chairpeople, CEOs, and senior leaders for the past 30 years. Guided by his purpose to "create a world better led," he focuses on CEO and board advisory coaching and consulting, specifically on improving leadership and talent, and transforming organizations through culture.

His experience spans a broad range of industries, including telecommunications, pharmaceuticals, aerospace, automotive, banking, consumer goods, and technology.

Over the years, Dustin has engaged with clients and led projects in more than 70 countries around the world. He is a widely recognized public speaker and has published numerous articles on leadership, talent, culture, and transformation. He is known as an influencer in corporate Europe and beyond.

Dustin began his career with Senn Delaney, a global consulting firm, becoming the youngest partner in the firm's history and managing partner for EMEA. He then joined Heidrick & Struggles to accelerate Senn Delaney's growth on a global platform. He has been managing partner for several firms' consulting practices, both regionally and globally.

A graduate of the University of California at Santa Barbara, Dustin earned a bachelor's degree in prelaw and economics. Dustin lives in London with his wife and two sons. He serves on the advisory board of Grassroots Soccer, a charity focused on improving the lives of young people across the African continent.

**Ed Manfre** is a trusted business leader, advisor, and accredited executive coach (ACC) with two decades of experience helping CEOs and C-Suite leaders energize and align their organizations for success. He has served in both executive and commercial leadership roles as a business builder and people leader. At the age of 38, he became one of the youngest partners in his firm's history.

Ed's clients include members of Fortune's "World's Best Places to Work" and "World's Most Admired Companies" lists. He has coached, advised, and consulted broadly across industries, from startups to the Fortune 100, including energy, financial services, professional services, healthcare, retail, pharmaceutical, technology, private equity, and nonprofit.

A sought-after public speaker and Telly Award–winning writer, Ed is a contributing author for the Forbes Human Resources Council, publishes frequent articles on leadership and organizational culture, and contributes as a board member to multiple private and not-for-profit organizations positively impacting their communities.

Ed earned an MBA from the University of Southern California (Marshall) and an undergraduate degree in communications from IUP. As a USC international fellow, he earned a certificate on doing business in the European Union from WHU—Otto Beisheim Graduate School of Management. He speaks English and German. Ed lives in Orange County, California, with his wife and two children.

# THE WORLD NEEDS YOUR LEADERSHIP.
## IT'S TIME TO THRIVE.

Create a calm center within yourself to navigate through whatever storms arise. Thriving will help you overcome whatever obstacles are in your path.

With a thriving life, you can enjoy:

+ Higher levels of performance in yourself and others
+ More satisfying, growth-focused experiences
+ Richer personal and professional relationships
+ More sustainable successes over the long term for an expanded network of stakeholders and communities

For more insight, resources, and activities to guide your journey of thriving, visit LeadThroughAnything.